POINT AND SHOOT

A Railway Photographic Memoir

Volume Two
Locomotives at work

TED READING

First published 2011
FINIAL PUBLISHING

ISBN 978-1-900467-47-6

Produced by Finial Publishing
15 Abingdon Drive, Caversham Park, Reading, RG4 6SA
Telephone: 01189-484103
Email: mail@finial.co.uk

Printed by Henry Ling Ltd, The Dorset Press, Dorchester, Dorset, DT1 1HD
Telephone: 01305 251066
www.henryling.co.uk

DEDICATION

IRIS READING

My original dedication to Iris in Volume One was for all her help, and for much more. It has to be said that without her enthusiasm to distribution of that book and all matters financial I would be in a pretty pickle and no mistake. Anyhow however successful (?) we may be with these books I have been told in no uncertain words . . . we will never make a profit. Nice to know who the boss is.

AUTHOR'S NOTE

As the title suggests this, my second book, comprises of train photographs which came a second to photographing in and around locomotive depots, the subject of Volume One. As both books cover the same period and are therefore linked I have included the original introduction 'The Author's Tale' and 'From Silver Halides to Pixels' in this volume. There is always the possibility that if you do not possess a copy of Point and Shoot Volume One, Locomotives on shed . . . you may just pop out and order one (ISBN 978-1-900467-45-2).

I would like to thank Peter Askey for allowing me to use his photographic collection and my elder brother Reg for proof-reading the Greenford article, and courtesy to the Northolt Model Railway Club for use of the photograph on the front cover.

THE AUTHOR'S TALE - FROM VOLUME ONE

Firstly, many thanks for buying my book, the first, hopefully, of a short series of photographic endeavours covering a twenty year span from the 1960s. I hope you will forgive my continual reference to motorcycles, this is an indulgence on my part but it fits in with the period covered by this book.

For want of a better year to start an introduction 1988 will do. I had rejoined the real working world after spending five years travelling up and down the countryside photographing railways whilst under the guise of working for a car leasing company.

My workmate and long time friend Paul Wells, then sadly died following a car accident and with his going a link with the past was lost. Over many years we had shared an interest in railways and motorcycles.

Ted, Peter, John and Paul,
Barry Dump, December 1975.

My enthusiasm over railways, well trainspotting, goes way back to the fifties. Starting work in 1961 as a laboratory assistant in the foundry trade my elder brother's hand-me-down moped came my way. This gave rise to a greater interest in motorbikes, eventually my only contact with railways being yearly 'lads day out' to Barry locomotive dump with long time chums Paul, Peter Askey and John Durrant. On meeting my Iris even the bikes took a bit of a back seat. Following on from a serious industrial accident in 1977 - I fell through the foundry roof - my interest in railways was reborn. In need of some drastic therapy, the body parts were not working too well, Iris encouraged me to get out and about, so eventually I wandered off photographing trains.

With interest redoubled more 'lads day outs' were organised revisiting old haunts and photographing, even then, a fast changing general railway scene.

These excursions proved shortlived as Paul loved driving but it was of the kind that could best be described as 'interesting'. He always managed to get into one scrape or another and eventually Peter and John thought the better of it, the final straw being a high speed dash down a Welsh mountain side.

However, I must have been of sterner stuff and carried on until Paul's untimely death and that really was an end to it. Not much fun by yourself.

Ted and Buster, Shelley Close,
Greenford c. 1955

There was some compensations as the family grew up - much to Iris and the children's dismay our holiday destinations always seemed to include a railway backdrop.

When, at their age back in the 1950s, any holiday with railway involvement, however tenuous, was looked upon by myself with great enthusiasm.

In early 1954, at the age of nine, the family moved to Greenford, West London, and thus on starting a new school one 'Buster', aka, Clive Featherstone, soon came my way. Buster was exciting, a leader of men, well of me at least. But for all the world we were two scruffy urchins that had by the age of ten or thereabouts mastered travelling around London and could navigate the Underground without adult assistance of any kind.

We were trainspotters, and for us our second home was Southall railway bridge spanning the former GW mainline out of Paddington.

By early 1959 Buster had decided it was time to spread our wings and that our meagre collection of train numbers would be dramatically increased by launching a full assault on the capital's loco sheds.

No easy prospect, so with pounding heart Willesden was the first attempted and over the Summer, armed with our London Transport Twin Rovers, we were pretty well chucked out, thrown out and ordered out of the Capital's loco sheds. Some of these establishments were near impregnable but by year's end we had bunked all that London had to offer, some many times over.

Ted, Feltham loco shed, December 1960, taken by Buster.

At some stage of the proceedings we both acquired pushbikes. Whilst Buster built up a state of the art Claud Butler lightweight racing job my dad did me proud by acquiring a gentleman's maroon Rudge. The thing weighed a ton, rod brakes, fully enclosed rear chain guard and, of course, a Sturmy Archer three speed gearing. For me a total embarrassment but you could, if money was short, just about heave it around London.

Train spotting opened our horizons with occasional train trips on our own as well as days out with Buster's parents and our own annual family holidays to Brighton. These were the highlights of a year, only somewhat blighted by the fact that Buster discovered I was half blind.

Not so good for a trainspotter who seemingly could not spot numbers unless he fell over the engine. This was something of a liability to the furtive spotter, not that I had realised it. As my eyesight seemingly deteriorated I gravitated to the front of the classroom and struggled to avoid the embarrassment and humiliating ridicule from classmates on having to wear National Health issue goggles. John Lennon came too late for me.

1960 dawned and disaster for Teddy.

Buster lost interest. Model Railways had taken him over and it wasn't long before his bedroom disappeared under layers of hardboard all supported by a Forth bridge style erection of 'two by one' timber. Worse was to follow, Buster left school and took up an engineering apprenticeship at Napiers, in Acton Vale, the manufacturer of Deltic engines.

Train spotting classmates were now thin on the ground as even Terry Bennet, best known as Ben, who you will come across if you read my next book, went off to join British Railways at West Ealing signal box.

Drastic measures were called for, the only other option being to join a club. Previously we had all frowned on this as we thought trainspotters clubs were for mummies boys, school cap, blazers, badges and all that sort of thing.

But by late 1960 I had joined The Home Counties Railway Club known to all as the 'Homo's'.

Trips with the 'Homo's' were a real eye opener. We were the boys equivalent of St. Trinians. For hockey sticks read notebooks and biros and you get the picture, I don't think the organisers ever had a permit between them

Whilst I carried on as before, Buster, even at school, was already toying with girls' affections and on starting work soon acquired a 650cc BSA Super Rocket.

But one last trip with Buster, a pushbike ride to Feltham Loco in late 1960, was to have a great impression on me and it wasn't his mum's cheese and cucumber sandwiches.

Buster, for the first time, toted a camera, or more a camera shaped object. It was cheap. It was plastic. It took pictures.

Our family had a camera. It was tatty old metal Box Brownie. We took it on holidays. Sometimes pictures would be seen, but only dad ever loaded film into the thing. Sometimes nothing ever came out.

Clive 'Buster' Featherstone, Shelley Close, Greenford 1961.

Photographs, so I thought, were for the wealthy. We did 'snaps' and 'snapping' trains hadn't really entered Teddy's head.

But Buster's snaps at Feltham made a great impression at school, most lads in those days didn't own cameras. Well not at our school, Brentside Secondary Modern Boys. Whilst the dog-eared copy of 'Lady Chatterlies Lover' did the rounds, pictures of trains or anything else were rarely seen.

The impact on me was immediate. The Box Brownie was commandeered, pocket money scraped together for a roll of Kodak 620 size film from Boots the Chemist and by the beginning of 1961 I was on my way to Old Oak Common. Mother was concerned, she seemed to view the camera as a family heirloom, dad, I think was glad to see the back of it. Back to Boots for processing and being much impressed would proudly show my snaps at school to anyone who would look at them. One young lad, Peter Askey, two years below me, showed an interest as both he and his dad, Frank, were keen on photography.

It wasn't long before introductions were made to the Askey family and Frank, Peter's father, was showing us the mysterious ways of darkroom lore.

When twenty pounds cash came my way and with very little in the way of forethought, or even consulting Frank, I rushed round to Boots and purchased a cheap 127 size plastic Kodak 44A camera box set. It even had a plastic clip on flash. On proudly showing my purchase to Frank and Peter they needless to say they were reduced to tears.

Home Counties Club trips accounted for the rest of the money so I had to put up with the camera. Still on a good sunny day the old 44A being of a largish 127 format could produce, for a beginner, a decent result. That is until the sun went in, then it was game over.

Ted will ill-fated Zenith and Mamiyaflex, Eastleigh loco shed, 25th August 1963.

On joining the working world I purchased some stylish heavy black-framed glasses then saved up for a camera, a 35mm Kodak Retinette 1A. Peter, on the other hand, had finally managed to prize Frank's camera away from him, a 120 size bellows Kershaw with Taylor Hobson lens, a great all British camera. This he used until the day he purchased a Minolta A5, a 35mm rangefinder jobby. Perhaps not so good but a lot cheaper to run. My Retinette 1A was eventually traded in for a Russian Fed-2, the word in the photographic magazines being, for the price, it had an excellent lens.

I think that it did, but the rest wasn't quite up to it. Mine started suffering from a focal plane shutter problem giving uneven exposure so it had to go. So thanks to the joys of hire purchase I went up in the world with a 120 size Mamiyaflex twin lens reflex. Brilliant though this camera was I was for ever running out of film and in those days even if you found a chemist shop open on a Sunday, they couldn't sell you a film. Even if you begged. A Russian Zenith SLR was purchased as a back up, not the world's best buy and dropping it on the floor didn't help, so both went for a 35mm Minolta SR1 single lens reflex.

However during this period events were rapidly overtaking us. Back in the fifties stored and dumped engines were relatively unknown other than at, as I recall, Nine Elms shed and at various locomotive works.

But by 1962 it all started to change. Willesden suddenly had two 'Princess' Pacifics in store which I couldn't believe. But this was a prelude of things to come as we began to witness the demise of

Paul Wells, Swindon Works,
5th July 1964.

steam. As the year ticked by every shed seemed to contain rapidly increasing numbers of withdrawn locos, the 'Kings' had gone by year's end and large swathes of Southern types went at a stroke.

The sudden demise of steam took us by surprise and as the number of withdrawn locos increased so did our of photographing of them. Also, at that age there were other things in life to interest us as well as railways. Worse still a total bias developed for the Western and Southern regions. It seemed better to photograph endless lines of dumped pannier tanks than to perhaps wander eastwards to record the demise of the 'other' regions. Even nature started to conspire against us, as trainspotters it was of no concern what the weather was doing but with photography in mind complete trips could be marred by dull, wet, unforgiving weather. On the transport front Peter had finally convinced mum and dad on the necessity of having a motorbike and by then we had met up with Paul and John, both two wheeled railway enthusiasts.

Paul was also keen on photography, yet another Kodak 44A.

Looking back my adventures with the 'Homo's' only lasted for just over a year. However they offered a varied itinerary even if, on occasions, there was little time to even get the camera out of its case. The four of us then continued shed bashing by train or motorbike and even occasionally with permits. As photography took preference things were done at a more leisurely pace even if, as the book title suggests, very much on the basis of 'point and shoot'. My picture taking spanned little more than four years. I was seventeen by the time I had progressed to the Mamiyaflex from the Box Brownie and was little over nineteen by the time it was all over.

To sum up, a visit to King's Cross Loco during the Summer of 1963 toting the Mamiflex produced a single A3, when last visited three years previous when Teddy was in full trainspotting mode it was a full house.

Although the demise of the steam locomotive caused me great sadness I am glad to have been around to witness some part of it. Whether the British Railways Modernisation plan had been implemented or not time was up for us and we had all moved on.

By the time of my roof escapade in 1977 when a somewhat incapacitated Teddy took to the trains again, the railways were in their 'blue' period, train numbers were all TOPS, and the steam engine was history.

Peter Askey, Old Oak Common, 24th January 1965.

FROM SILVER HALIDES TO PIXELS

On reflection this book owes a lot to Frank Askey. Although a amateur photographer he was very professional in his outlook and I doubt I would have progressed much past the box camera stage without him. Another factor was that unable to afford better photographic equipment on my wages my parents would sign hire purchase agreements on my behalf.

Buying my first 35mm camera I initially used Ilford HP3 400ASA film but through the Summer of 1962, I underwent a photographic learning curve. This was not a good time for doing this. Buying film in bulk was a sound option, but ex-MOD film was not such a good idea nor was trying high speed films. All generally gave poor, or in a few cases, disastrous results. Eventually I settled down to 125ASA FP3 and a second hand Weston exposure meter was purchased replacing a simple plastic dial-up device. Processing was done round at the Askey's home in the kitchen, films were loaded up in the dark under the stairs. Fine grain developers Promicrol and Microdol were used with high speed fixers which greatly reduced processing times. Printing pictures was exceedingly time consuming and required great skill, thus developing films then outstripped printing and both Peter and myself eventually built up huge backlog of negatives. These were then initially stored in a haphazard way and it was not until later that all the negatives were placed into albums. By then some of the early ones had gone missing, for example very few Midland region negatives survive prior to 1963.

Two house moves, and some forty years later my eldest son presented me with a stand alone 35mm scanner/printer. Actually he didn't present it to me, he purchased it on a whim and then sold it to me knowing I had an interest in digital scanning. He was not wrong. However within six months the retail price had dropped by fifty quid, then another fifty and within another six months it vanished off the radar screen. Such is technology. My initial efforts showed some promise but attempting BW printing on a colour printer has its limitations. But by trial and error and using professional photographic papers reasonable results were produced. At this stage there was no thought of a book but two factors then came together which not only improved print quality but put the thoughts of a book in my mind.

Elder son then took pity and gave us a lap top. However to fully explain its workings we had to tie him to a chair to stop him escaping. Shortly after this Iris signed me up for a one day course on digital imaging. This introduced me to Picasa, a free download from Google, and it has to be said I never looked back, even purchasing another scanner catering for large format negatives. At that stage the old enlarger, lenses etc finally came down from the attic and went to the car boot.

Then in 2008 events took a dramatic turn, a railway package holiday to the Hartz mountains introduced us to one fellow traveller John Villers, a publisher of books.

Not only a publisher of books, but one with a great interest in railways who lives in striking distance of home. Approaching John about doing a book he agreed to take on the project, for that is what it has been. Without his help and encouragement this book would never have happened and I would not have spent the past few years living under the stairs with two scanners and a lap top in a state of mortal fear waiting for a systems crash. I have even became conversant with a memory stick. Forty years on and I'm back under the stairs again simply because we live in a very small house, but at least with the new technology I have light.

Setting the book up picture wise has taken considerable time and at this stage I must thank Peter for allowing me the use of his own negative collection not only for this book but, should it see the light of day, the next, 'Steam on the Move'. On Paul's death I inherited his negative collection so it pleases me to include some of his 44A Plastic camera shots. At the time Paul had his own priorities, and that was buying a Honda 250 and not a better camera.

My thanks go to Clive 'Buster' Featherstone for helping me get some order into the events of fifty years past and passing a critical eye over my ramblings and also to Neville Bridger of Nevis Books for filling my attic with countless railway journals of the 1960s so that I may appear more knowledgeable than what I really am.

I have to say that the pictorial quality is more old approach than the 'new approach' of railway photography in the mid 1960s, but although all the negatives have been digitally scanned, other than negative imperfections removed, what you see is what you get. Of technical interest 35mm negs have been scanned at 2400dpi and 120 size at 1200dpi.

TRAINS OF THOUGHT - THOUGHTS OF TRAINS

My first ever photograph was of 'Hall' class No.5973 on a parcels train running past South Greenford Halt on a cold January day in 1961. This windswept halt is set high on a embankment and was our local branch line running from Greenford to Ealing Broadway. More importantly it was a loop connecting the former GW Birmingham to the Swindon main lines. Therefore it was a busy through route but the branch lost its '14xx' auto tank and trailer to DMU stock back in 1958. Even so it would play its part in our childhood memories, on school sports days Buster and I would dodge any sporting activities, lie down on the grass and idly watch said tank locos, usually Nos.1421 or 1474, puff past sometimes being sat between its two coaches. On the other hand Iris as a young child would travel with mum to go shopping at Ealing and was petrified of our little tank loco and would hide in the darkest corner of the halt's corrugated metal pagoda hut. This must have been the last act of desperation, Great Western halts had no toilet facilities and so it followed that such dark corners always substituted as the gentlemen's loo! Likewise a certain trainspotter's first sexual fumblings were attempted under said pagoda, not mine I hasten to add, only to find the female deception for stuffing one's bra with socks. I fumbled much later and elsewhere. Whatever, on that cold January day in 1961 I had stopped there for a while whilst on a pushbike ride to

Ted's first ever photograph.

Old Oak Common with the family Box Brownie tucked firmly away in the bike's saddle bag. Teddy went trainspotting, that meant shed bashing and the camera went along for the ride . . . and taking anything other than locomotive snaps on shed was never contemplated, judging by my first and only effort at photographing a moving train. Trouble was I had high expectations and after looking through Eric Treacy's superb railway books and then Frank Askey's action railway shots taken on holiday in Cornwall, completely put me in my place. At least I had a good excuse in that my box camera was only just suitable for still shots and even then only with the help of the sun. As we shall see, at about the same time, a young Paul Wells had other ideas about the potential use of a box camera.. Not that I knew him at that time. My pragmatic approach to photography never really changed even with the purchase of 35mm cameras. I still shied away from photographing moving trains, even those that took us on shed bashing excursions. By 1963 Peter Askey dragged me screaming and shouting away from my beloved engine sheds to the lineside. Things were changing fast, main line steam was in quick decline, and if it was not for Peter there simply wouldn't be enough pictures to publish this book. Frank swapped his 120 format Kershaw for a 35mm Minolta in the summer of 1962, and for this reason we all trooped off to King's Cross station to try out our cameras. During the early 1960s many professional and amateur photographers still used large format cameras, the smaller 35mm format being looked down on or at least viewed by some with great suspicion as not being up to the job. Unless it was a Leica. Frank's photographs have the privilege of leading this book off, he was certainly impressed with his new purchase, but for the larger picture perhaps the 120 format had it . . . and as for me, using 35mm colour transparency film for the first time, even with its slow film speed and poor exposure latitude, resulted in eventual disaster. On inspecting them many years later they had sadly badly deteriorated and were useless.

Even 35mm black and white photography had its problems with the vexed subject of film grain never far away. Using fast film had its advantages for moving train shots but any degree of negative cropping at the printing stage on a train that's a dot on the horizon would give terrible grainy results. A few of my early efforts of action photography have survived to be included in this book but most landed in the bin, where some of the more discerning of you might conclude would be the best place for them. Grainy pictures, or even blurry box camera pictures, can now be viewed as acceptable when of archival value or even have artistic merit. Pity that, didn't realise I was doing history or anything remotely artistic in my young day. With 35mm format I soon realised that with moving train photography you really had to be spot on in picture taking. Still my second 35mm camera a Russian made Fed 2, at least had a 1/500th shutter speed, even though the viewfinder could only be described as pathetic which also included a just about discernable rangefinder.

Knowing when to press the shutter was more a matter of luck than judgement. The real leather camera case also had a problem, a very strange smell to it . . . like the cow was still alive and functioning.

Action photography improved slightly with the arrival of the large format twin lens reflex. I had convinced myself that looking down at the reversed image on the fresnel screen concentrated the mind wonderfully on the subject matter. In recent times looking at the number of static loco shots on shed with posts sticking up out of chimney pots I'm not so sure. It wasn't so much that the actual taking of a fast moving train improved, more the forgiving nature of such a large negative format gave me room to manoeuvre some forty five years later at the scanning stage. When viewing superb action photographs of the top railway photographers from this period I show a good deal of respect for the 35mm man, even if he used a Leica.

Purchasing my first 35mm single-lens reflex made my photography a great deal easier. A lightweight camera, easy to use, 'on board' exposure metering, a clear viewfinder, easy focussing and the simple but wonderful fact that what you clearly saw was what you got. At last I was finally able to photograph a moving train and manage a moderate size print Then six months later, by January 1965, we had all done with railways and the within the year the camera had gone to help finance motorbike racing and shortly after that I met Iris. Things happen quick at that age. In many ways we never really shook off the culture of shed bashing, many photographs presented here are the result of one day motorbike excursions to the lineside, then never to return. Trespassing on railway property meant nothing to us which is a good thing in the sense that otherwise I would hardly have taken any photographs. Having said that, perhaps more railway station shots might have been attempted which in retrospect is the one thing I now wish I had done

The chap second on the right bent over his camera is me . . . seemingly photographing the train in the wrong direction!

PAUL WELLS AND THE BOX CAMERA, ART OR RUBBISH?

On preparing Volume One a few of my own and Paul's early box camera photos were included, mostly acceptable but with a couple of 'iffy' ones simply to illustrate a loco. Paul started railway photography at about the same time as myself and used, as did I, a Kodak 44A Brownie box camera. This he used mostly through our spotting days occasionally supplementing it with a decrepit old pre-war 620 format Kodak bellows camera, of which a panned photo of a 'West Country' class appears on the front cover.

Kodak 44A camera.

Being two years younger than myself Paul's pocket money didn't run to better cameras and on starting work motor bikes had became a greater passion. Eventually owning a 305 Honda this could be an expensive passion. It had to be said that holding his own on the Japanese lightweight against British 650's was commendable stuff, the downside being he spent more than his fair share riding pillion with the rest of us. So money for cameras just was not there, but when it came to using his camera Paul knew no boundaries. Whereas I shied away from experimenting, Paul was constantly attempting the impossible with varying degrees of failure. Peter Askey and myself met up with Paul during 1963 and thought ourselves superior in both the camera and motorbike departments.. At the time Paul's transport was a 50cc NSU Quickly moped with its handlebars upside down for less wind resistance and greater speed. Desperate stuff. Even more desperate was his camera and motley collection of attempted action shots. These it had to be said caused great amusement . . . well ridicule actually. Whilst any degree of high speed blur in our efforts would mostly result in rejection Paul obviously took a more liberal view. If ever there was a Bloomsbury School of railway photography, Paul was your man. The subject matter was attempted from all angles, classic three quarter - touch of the

A 'Castle' near Hanger Lane c.1961/2.

Eric Treacy here - panning, and head on. Nothing deterred our Paul, and all at 1/30th of a second. It has to be said that the 44A Instruction book advised practice at moving shots and even then only at a fair distance. Like half a mile perhaps.

However, near fifty years on, and with the job of sorting pictures for this book, I went back to Paul's collection and my heart warmed to them. Well some of them. Technically as poor as ever, in fact more so, but some have grown on me. They have a pictorial quality about them. Even artistic. A couple of Paul's action shots appear in the book, some are reproduced here and, as said, one is on the front cover. I like them, and although Paul hung on to his box camera for far too long I wish I had taken on his train of thought, and what do they say now, opened the envelope.

A 'King' near Ealing Broadway c.1961/2.

Plate 1. No.60003 *Andrew.K.McCosh*   July 1962   F.Askey - Minolta SR3

Plate 2. No 61179   July 1962   F.Askey - Minolta SR3

King's Cross station on a sunny Sunday morning in July1962. Save for a few corridor door ends scattered about there is little company as King's Cross allocated 'B1' No.61179 pulls out shortly followed by 'A4' No.60003 *Andrew K McCosh*. She has more than enough coal in her tender and a great oil slick down her sleek front end, no doubt due to over oiling a smoke box door hinge. English Electric Type 4 diesels were introduced in late 1958 and the 'Deltics' in 1961 but steam was not eliminated until 1964 being kept busy on parcel, relief, and sleeper workings.

Plate 3. No.60111 *Enterprise*   July 1962   F.Askey - Minolta SR3

Plate 4. No.60111 *Enterprise*   July 1962   F.Askey - Minolta SR3

Two views of King's Cross as 'A3' No.60111 *Enterprise* fitted with German style smoke deflectors pulls past the classic signal box and colour light signalling heading for the Gas Works Tunnels. Photographed from King's Cross, York Road station, used only for southbound local trains, she was noted for some fine running and on one occasion during August 1962 trying to cut back 100 minutes lost by a failed 'Deltic'. Diesel failures were not uncommon throughout this transitional period but this would not save her and she was withdrawn by year's end.

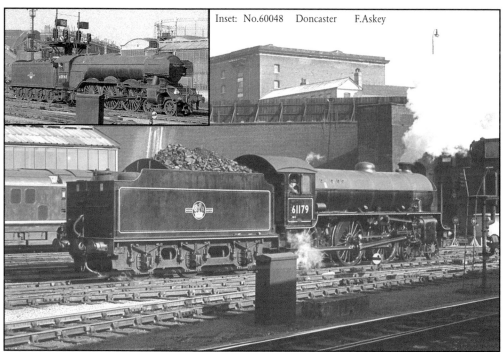

Inset: No.60048   Doncaster   F.Askey

Plate 5. No.61179   July 1962   F.Askey - Minolta SR3

Plate 6. No.60085 *Manna*   July 1962   F.Askey - Minolta SR3

There would be many light engine movements between King's Cross 'Top Shed' and the terminus. On our visit class 'B1' No.61179 rolls past the stabling point for her next duty followed by (inset) 'A3' No.60048 *Doncaster* also fitted with German style smoke deflectors. The majority of the class were so fitted following on from receiving double chimneys towards the end of their working lives. Meanwhile another class 'A3' No.60085 *Manna* has finished her turn and backs off for the loco shed. Note the old chap wearing his cheese-cutter or flat cap, common to that generation of working men but outmoaded for a younger generation.

Plate 7. No.6018 *King Henry VI*   F.Askey -Minolta SR3

Plate 8. No.6018 *King Henry VI*   F.Askey -Minolta SR3

The Stephenson Locomotive Society organised the 'SLS Special' Birmingham and return last 'King' run on the 28th April 1963. No.6018 pulled the train comprising of twelve coaches grossing 440 tons and reportedly touched 90mph in places. The train is on the Greenford loop which connected the Birmingham and Swindon main lines. The photographs are taken between Castle Bar and Drayton Green halts. Such a view today is impossible as the cutting has now been totally covered over and a housing estate built across the top. Love the inspector in the cab with the trilby hat having his last ride.

Plate 9. Morning departure to the West　　6th September 1964　　Minolta SR1

Plate 10. 4.15pm Paddington departure late 1964　　P.Wells - Halina 35mm

An unidentified 'Warship' stands at Paddington station on an Exeter bound train and I'll be off bashing the local engine sheds and then back home via Taunton. The ladies strolling down the platform seem in casual conversation, perhaps they had inspected the new diesel traction prior to boarding the train. Or not. The bottom picture has Paul Wells and myself, late on in 1964, riding the 4.15 out of Paddington to Bicester. Hauled by 'Grange' class No.6853 we are pulling past the long Platform One with an interesting rake of parcel stock. The photograph is Paul's, of mine there is no trace.

Plate 11. No.1500   Mamiya C22

Plate 12. No.1506   Mamiya C22

The '15xx' pannier tanks appeared in 1949 after Nationalisation. Compared to the run-of-the-mill GW pannier tanks they were of unusual appearance and even more so for having outside cylinders and Walschaerts valve gear. The majority spent their working lives located at Old Oak Common on Paddington ECS duties. I caught these two coming in to pick up empty stock, the driver in the bottom photo gave me a wave, but I missed it. I was off to Swindon for the day and was glad I photographed them because by year's end they had been withdrawn.

Plate 13. No.8436   Minolta SR1

Plate 14. No.8459   Minolta SR1

Two more views of Paddington's panniers, this time the '94xx' Class. One of No.8436's crew is relaxing reading his newspaper between duties. Note the non-standard front number plate and, as with Plate 11 opposite, the original track work at the station throat. Of the bottom picture one of No.8459's crew seems even more relaxed and discussing something with his mate. I, on the other hand, seem only to photograph pannier tanks when at Paddington, this picture being taken at the end of Platform One. These two were withdrawn in June 1965 and the class became extinct.

Plate 15. 4.15pm Paddington departure   P.Wells - Halina 35mm

Plate 16. 4.15pm Paddington departure   P.Wells - Halina 35mm

Back to Paul Wells, myself and the 4.15 from Paddington. This was to be the only scheduled steam working out of Paddington until 11th June 1965 when the service became dieselised and steam finally bowed out of Paddington. Paul and I decided to take a ride sometime late in 1964 and the top view shows the extensive goods yards at Westbourne Park with a Paddington bound DMU whilst in the bottom picture we are about to dive under the Great Western Road bridge with Westbourne Park station behind.

Plate 17. No.6165   6th September 1964   Minolta SR1

Plate 18. No.D1027 *Western Lancer*   12th July 1964   Minolta SR1

The top picture has '61xx' class No.6165, shunting alongside Kensal Green gasworks which made a distinctive backdrop to the railway till it closed in the 1970s and the site eventually cleared. Meanwhile our '61xx' has lost her front numberplate giving her a more traditional Great Western look whilst the driver or fireman appears to be waving good bye to our train driver. Meanwhile within a mile to the west of Kensal Green gasworks is Paddington bound 'Western' class diesel No.D1027 with the flyover embankment for ECS duties in the background.

Plate 19. 'King' class   c.1961/62   P.Wells - Kodak 44A

Plate 20. No.7023 *Penrice Castle*   21st. July 1963   Mamiya C22

Two views of Mitre Bridge which took Scrubs Lane Road and the West London Railway over the main Western Region running lines. Both pictures show Paddington bound trains. Paul Wells' box camera has caught a fast moving 'King' to good effect. The driver of this train is clearly still making time but I fancy a shutter speed of 1/30th sec has made for a more dramatic effect. On the other hand the bottom picture, a 'Castle' hauled Worcester train taken at 1/500th sec, although technically a better picture lacks any of the drama of the top picture.

Plate 21. No.9418   August 1964   Minolta SR1

Inset: No.6016 *King Edward V*   c.1961/2   P.Wells

Plate 22. No.3754   21st. July 1963   Mamiya C22

By 1963 express steam workings on the Western Region were few and far between with only the Worcester/ Hereford service remaining, the only regular steam offerings left were the ECS duties. The top view has '94xx' class No.9418 heading for Paddington whilst the bottom shows '57xx' class No.3754 about to go under Mitre Bridge for Old Oak carriage sidings. The inset photo predates the other two by a year or so and shows that even the mighty 'Kings' have to muck in with the lower orders. Not to the taste of Gordon the Big Engine then.

Plate 23. No.9706   August 1964   Minolta SR1

Plate 24. No.9706   August 1964   Minolta SR1

Two photographs of '57xx' Condensing tank loco No.9706. Whilst the top view shows the loco on the spur from the West London Line the bottom was taken later whilst the train was being shunted, its ultimate destination now long forgotten. Eleven of these condensing tanks were built for working the London Transport running lines between Paddington and Smithfield market. All were allocated to and withdrawn from Old Oak Common. By the time of these pictures, August 1964, three remained and No.9706 was the last to be withdrawn in December 1964.

Plate 25. 'Western' class arrival   August 1964   Minolta SR1

Plate 26. No.D1720   12th July 1964   Minolta SR1

By late 1963 both diesel hydraulic and diesel electric traction were well established on the Western Region. The Sulzer diesel electrics had displaced the 'Western' class hydraulics from the Birmingham main line by the summer. An unidentified 'Western' class diesel hydraulic passes under Mitre Bridge on a Paddington bound express whilst Sulzer diesel electric No.D1720 was light engine having worked its turn and was running back to Old Oak Common

OLD OAK COMMON JUNCTION - 1st. JUNE 1963

Plate 27. No.7025 *Sudeley Castle*   Mamiya C22

Plate 28. No.7032 *Denbigh Castle*   Mamiya C22

With the summer of 1963 the Hereford and Worcester route was the last main line steam service out of Paddington. This was soon to change as 'Hymek' class diesel hydraulics were introduced during July and had taken over by September, although diesel failures were commonplace with steam working into 1964. The 'Castle' class final swansong on this service is caught at Old Oak Common Junction in June 1963 with No.7025 *Sudeley Castle* working a Down train whilst sister loco No.7032 *Denbigh Castle* is working an Up parcels.

Plate 29. No.3646   3rd August 1963   Mamiya C22

Plate 30. No.9725   29th September 1962   Fed -2

These two pictures show '57xx' panniers at work up at the throat of Old Oak Common carriage sidings and loco shed where they joined the main line. Not normally an area where trainspotters would go. '57xx' class No.3646 complete with shunter's wagon works the litter strewn carriage sidings. I sometimes used to think the cleaners simply swept the rubbish out of the carriage door onto the ground outside. Meanwhile No.9725 is working empty wagons out of the loco yard and in the background is an old grounded carriage used as a railway workers bothy and storeroom.

Plate 31. No.31913   1st. June 1963   Mamiya C22

Plate 32. No.7033 *Hartlebury Castle*   26th August 1962   Fed-2

Southern interloper 'W' class tank No.31913 shunts some wagons at Old Oak Common Junction close to the site of the old Great Western halt which closed in 1947 and by 1963 there was no trace. And that is as far as our 'W' went. 1962 saw few action shots even with 35mm equipment and 'Castle' class No.7033 *Hartlebury Castle* was caught slowing down to stop at Ealing Broadway station. The GW station buildings at road level had been demolished two years earlier and it would be several years later before the new Ealing Broadway station would finally emerge.

EALING BROADWAY - 14th JANUARY 1962

Plate 33. No.4089 *Donnington Castle*   Fed-2

Plate 34. LT Underground Stock   Fed-2

Again Ealing Broadway station. This was on a cold frosty morning in January 1962 and I was off to Swindon for the day. The train engine was 'Castle' class No.4089 *Donnington Castle*. This quick unplanned shot includes London Transport silver 1959 Central Line stock with doors left wide open for passenger discomfort and District Line 'R' stock in the middle distance. At that time Ealing Broadway comprised of three separate stations, the bottom picture has again Central Line silver 1959 stock alongside the District Line station with 'K' stock of 1927 vintage.

Plate 35. No.5914 *Ripon Hall*   24th July 1963   Mamiya C22

Inset: West Ealing Station and yards.   c.1961/2   P.Wells

Plate 36. No.8459   24th July 1963   Mamiya C22

On passing West Ealing I stopped to look around the station's milk dock. These negatives are missing but those of the two steam locos to pass by, 'Hall' class No.5914 *Ripon Hall* and '94xx' pannier No.8459 remain. The 'Hall' runs light engine whilst the pannier is running on the Up Main line with a freight. These set 'timepiece' photos are at odds with the newly installed colour light signalling equipment. The inset picture taken from Jacobs Ladder footbridge, West Ealing, a year or so earlier shows the goods yard and signal box where my chum Ben worked on leaving school.

Plate 37. No.7005 *Sir Edward Elgar*   8th August 1963   Mamiya C22

Plate 38. No.7027 *Thornbury Castle*   26th June 1963   P.Askey - Minolta A5

Two views of 'Castle' hauled Paddington bound express trains. 'Castle' class No.7005 *Sir Edward Elgar*, top picture, approaches Hanwell station, the other being No.7027 *Thornbury Castle* passing by the rear of Southall loco shed yards. Note, in the foreground, the 20mph restriction for the crossing from the Down Main line. At that time Hanwell station was fully staffed and boasted a proper booking office. The platform buildings were in poor condition even then but the station retained most of its large Great Western wooden station signs, something it would do for many years.

Plate 39. Rear of Southall Loco Shed   5th July 1964   Minolta SR1

Plate 40. Southall Loco Shed and yards   26th August 1962   Fed-2

Southall Loco shed as viewed from the train. The top picture shows the rear of the shed yard and small repair shop, note the cars parked in the shed yard and the goods depot, middle distance, which was was sold to Quaker Oats Ltd. In the lower picture can be seen the empty pushbike racks at the entrance. The loco shed was closed to steam in 1965 but remained open for diesel multiple units for many years. 'Hall' class No.4987 (top inset) is acting as a stationary boiler which I was once allowed to fire and the passing 'Castle' (lower inset) displays its large smokebox mounted headcode something which would soon be discontinued.

SOUTHALL

Plate 41. No.4979 *Wootton Hall*   14th July 1963   Mamiya C22

Plate 42. No.9726   8th August 1963   Mamiya C22

Two 1963 views of Southall station and the Brentford branch. 'Hall' class No.4979 *Wootton Hall* is slowly pulling through with an Up parcels train on the Slow, or Relief, running lines. In the middle distance, behind the station is Southall Gas Works with two of Southall's greatest landmarks. The brick clad water tower was built in 1890 and known locally as 'Southall's Castle' and immediately behind is the 1930s gasometer. In the bottom picture '57xx' class No.9726 heads up a goods train on the Brentford branch passing, in the background, the giant Quaker Oats concern.

Plate 43. No.2899   11th August 1963   P.Askey - Minolta A5

Plate 44. No.4703   8th August 1963   Mamiya C22

Just east of Southall station a pedestrian footbridge spans the main running lines and associated sidings. For many this short cut over the railway saved a long walk round by the station. Mid way across the bridge and just south of the main running lines was a gated spur, always unlocked, which gave railway staff access to the loco shed down a flight of wooden steps. With the bridge spur visible No.2899 is caught on the Down Main running lines whilst '47xx' class No.4703 works empty passenger stock on the Up Relief lines under the footbridge.

Plate 45. Nos.7006 *Lydford Castle* & 6988 *Swithland Hall*   21st. July 1963   Mamiya C22

Plate 46. Nos.7006 *Lydford Castle* & 6988 *Swithland Hall*   21st. July 1963   Mamiya C22

Double headers through Southall were not so common and No.7006 *Lydford Castle* coupled to No.6988 *Swithland Hall* deserve two pictures. Note the three young children with their fathers watching the progress of our train as it passes by underneath the footbridge. What a memory. Back in the 1950s hoards of trainspotters would mull around Southall's footbridge wooden steps. Mass confusion would occur if Down expresses, double headed, with smoke box route headboards fitted stormed past. In the resulting chaos the second loco generally went unrecorded.

Plate 47. No.7023 *Penrice Castle* July 1963 Mamiya C22

Plate 48. No.5018 *St. Mawes Castle* 8th August 1963 Mamiya C22

Two 'Castles' photographed from Southall's footbridge. No.7023 *Penrice Castle* heads a Worcester express on the Down Main line whilst No.5018 *St. Mawes Castle* is on a lesser duty, a goods train on the Up Relief line. My spotting days started at Jacobs Ladder footbridge, West Ealing in the mid 1950s but the local Teddy Boys would sometimes push you about and worse still throw your 'ABCs' down to the tracks below. At Southall you were secure amongst your own. All short trousers, sandwiches and bottles of pop, but don't ever recall seeing cameras.

Plate 49. No.6959 *Peatling Hall*   25th July 1963   Mamiya C22

Plate 50. No.6983 *Otterington Hall*   14th July 1963   Mamiya C22

'Modified Hall' No.6959 *Peatling Hall* runs past on an Up goods passing Southall's extended goods depot while fellow classmate No.6983 *Otterington Hall* just manages to get exposed on the end of the film, that's all there is. Note the articulated trailer just caught by the camera in the goods yard. For myself that bridge at Southall was my second home till the late 1950s when Buster's master shed bashing plan was put into effect. Only Peter Askey's determination for moving shots brought me back in 1963, but the best had gone and we just caught steam in the nick of time.

Plate 51. No.4979 *Wootton Hall*   14th July 1963   P.Askey - Minolta A5

Plate 52. No.7910 *Hown Hall*   18th May 1963   Mamiya C22

Down at track level Peter caught 'Hall' No.4979 *Wootton Hall* passing the goods depot on the same train as I had photographed in Plate 41 steaming through the station. Meanwhile I just about manage to photograph 'Modified Hall' No.7910 *Hown Hall* on a Down goods train. Well I failed with the train but at least caught the locomotive. During 1963 GW locos generally seemed to retain their name and number plates, within a year this would change with plates being removed and some even losing brass safety valve covers.

Plate 53. Nos.D3996 & D847 *Strongbow*   Mamiya C22

Plate 54. No.7922 *Salford Hall*   Mamiya C22

A diesel failure, caught on camera. Not uncommon in those days. On this occasion 'Warship' class No.D847 *Strongbow* has failed or struggled onto Southall where shunter D3996 runs out to pull the 'Warship' off into the loco shed while 'Modified Hall' No.7922 *Salford Hall* is summoned to take over. One can almost hear the coughing and wheezing as she starts off. I cannot date the colour light signalling but in earlier days I recall being able to tell when express trains were due by watching long distant semaphore signals and listening to bell codes ringing in the signal box.

Inset: Paul's quick shot of a double-headed milk train.

Plate 55. No.D803 *Albion*   11th August 1963   P.Askey - Minolta A5

Plate 56. 'Warship' class   July 1964   Minolta SR1

The new...ish order. Two 'Warships' on Down trains photographed a year apart. No.D803 *Albion* one of the original builds with route identification discs and, as yet, no yellow warning panel heads a parcels containing a interesting assortment of rolling stock whilst, a year later, an unidentified 'Warship' is caught on a Bristol express. Careful examination of the colour light signalling will show that over the year some of the original equipment has gone. Note the single parcel unit DMU parked up the loco shed head shunt. In earlier days this would have been a Great Western railcar.

Plate 57. No.D1055 *Western Advocate*   11th May 1963   P.Askey - Minolta A5

Plate 58. 'Hymek' class   11th May 1963   P.Askey - Minolta A5

Taken from the footbridge proper showing the spur whose steps lead down to the asbestos hut where lived the 'Authority', the disused original coaler/water tank, water softener and loco shed proper. 'Western' class No.D1055 *Western Advocate* passes on a Down Cardiff express with only three spotters present and even these have gone when an unidentified 'Hymek' rolls past. A chap once appeared on the footbridge with the bottom half of a submarine periscope. We all took turns supporting it and looking through the eyepiece towards the loco shed. I remember being extremely impressed not by its magnification but by its clarity.

Plate 59. No.6018 *King Henry VI*   Mamiya C22

Plate 60. No.6018 *King Henry VI*   Mamiya C22

The Stephenson Locomotive Societies' Last 'King' Run on the 28th April 1963 as seen previously on Plates 7 & 8 running down the Greenford loop. The train halted at Southall for some time prior to going onto Swindon for a visit to the railway works before finally returning to Birmingham. Why the train stopped at Southall I have no idea but it was on the Down Main and so gave a chance to take some last photographs. The top photograph should not be attempted on a normal running day, but I bet some have tried to get near to it. The goods yard, however, looks more than busy.

Plate 61. No.6018 *King Henry VI*   P.Askey - Minolta A5

Inset: Health & Safety, eat your heart out!

Plate 62. No.6018 *King Henry VI*   P.Askey - Minolta A5

'King' class No.6018 *King Henry VI* is about to start off again and pass under the footbridge and Southall East station signal box. but not before Peter runs the length of the station platform to get a fine view of her passing under the station road bridge. Homage has been paid by us enthusiasts, see inset, with little respect for our own safety, although I'm pleased to say, but not surprised, that no deaths or serious injury took place. However No.6018, one of the last to be withdrawn in December 1962, died the death of a thousand cuts some five months later. Or did she? Ho,ho.

Plate 63. No.6018 *King Henry VI*   F.Askey - Minolta SR3

Plate 64. No.6018 *King Henry VI*   Mamiya C22

Our 'King' picks up speed leaving Southall station with its French chateau style towers behind. There were three of these elegant structures but one out of view was demolished at about this time. The bottom picture sums it all up. The 'King' now steams into history. The track gangers stand bemused, the old fellow on the signal gantry and the mother placing her beloved child on the running lines tells us its another age. And on the sidings alongside the gasometer I once saw, many years previous, a 'Dukedog' shunting old wooden private owner wagons. My best cop ever.

Plate 65. No.4705   P.Askey - Minolta A5

Plate 66. No.4920 *Dumbleton Hall*   P.Askey- Minolta A5

Running past Southall gas works on the Down Relief lines are '47xx' class No.4705 on a car transporter train, note the Ford Cortina Mk 1, and 'Hall' class No.4920 *Dumbleton Hall* on a milk train. Southall gas works covered some 90 acres and during the mid 1960s new gas production processes were put in rendering its internal railway system and little saddle tanks redundant. The whole plant was closed in the 1970s, its buildings and infrastructure remaining derelict for many years and becoming a suitable home for TV programmes such as Doctor Who, The Sweeney, The Professionals, etc.

Plate 67. No.7032 *Denbigh Castle*   26th July 1963   Mamiya C22

Plate 68. No.7033 *Hartlebury Castle*   26th August 1962   Fed-2

Hayes, Middlesex, had a large industrial manufacturing base mainly situated to the north of the GW main line. 'Castle' class No.7032 *Denbigh Castle* on a Worcester train passes the EMI plant, one of the largest companies in the area. By 1963 smokebox mounted route head boards had been discontinued but the practise remained by chalking the route description on the smokebox door. Another 'Castle', No.7033 *Hartlebury Castle* approaches Slough station which, in August 1962, retains semaphore signalling although local services by this time were in the hands of DMUs.

Plate 69. No.5986 *Arbury Hall*   2nd December 1962   Fed-2

Plate 70. Slough Loco Shed   19th July 1964   Minolta SR1

A cold winter's day at Slough station with 'Hall' class No.5986 *Arbury Hall* running through with a parcels on the Up Relief lines. The year is 1962. Again note the semaphore signals which would soon be gone and the newly constructed replacement road bridge spanning the main running lines. Of the road trailers on the Up platform I have no idea. Slough loco shed as viewed from a Down train in July 1964. The depot had closed the month before but still retains a diesel shunter whilst DMUs are stabled opposite on the other side of the Windsor branch running lines.

Plate 71. Class 28xx *loco*   19th July 1964   Minolta SR1

Plate 72. No.30850 *Lord Nelson*   24th June 1962   F.Askey - Minolta SR3

Pictured by train as per Plate 70, we have a unidentified '28xx' class just west of Slough on a ballast train. Our loco is bereft of front number plate and no front lamps. Note the colour light signalling.

Taplow station on 24th June 1962 saw Frank and Peter Askey and myself photographing the Home Counties Railway Club's Swindon special, hauled by No.30850 *Lord Nelson*. As we were there I think we hung around for a while, 'the ladies' waited in the car. Frank's new 35mm camera features here, Peter used dad's old Kershaw, my efforts were all under exposed.

Plate 73. No.7004 *Eastnor Castle*   F.Askey - Minolta SR3

Plate 74. No.6966 *Witchingham Hall*   F.Askey - Minolta SR3

These two pictures show Taplow station's Down Main and Up Slow, or Relief. 'Castle' class No.7004 *Eastnor Castle* heads a Down express and shows the west side of the station with small goods yard, period cast iron warning signs and stationary carriage. However we just caught the semaphore signals as they were replaced by colour lights over the coming months. Looking the other way towards Reading, 'Modified Hall' No.6966 *Witchingham Hall* with a full head of steam swings through on an Up parcels train, the leading vehicle being a Southern Railway parcels or utility van.

Plate 75. 'Warship' class loco   F.Askey - Minolta SR3

Plate 76. 'Warship' class loco   F.Askey - Minolta SR3

Luckily for us Frank Askey was an amateur photographer and not a railway enthusiast and to him a diesel hauled train was as interesting as any other. Looking back some fifty years on I'm glad he did. For some reason I though Frank was noting the engine numbers, on asking him later he replied, "Why would I be writing down train numbers?". Fair point. Both pictures feature 'Warships', the top on a west of England express, the loco not yet having received its small yellow warning ends, whilst the lower shows the station's topiary to maximum effect as an Up express passes by.

Plate 77. 'Warship' class loco   F.Askey - Minolta SR3

Plate 78. 'Hymek' class loco   F.Askey - Minolta SR3

Again both trains, 'Warship' and 'Hymek' powered have not received their small yellow warning ends. These were introduced early in 1962 and within a short period all diesels would be so treated. The signal to the immediate right of the 'Warship' would, I think, be for the Down Relief. Due to GW engines being right hand drive, and not as other railway companies, signals could be placed in odd positions. In the lower picture the leading coach behind the Hymek appears to be of Great Western origin as the train passes under the station's 1884 lattice iron footbridge.

TAPLOW - 24th JUNE 1962

Plate 79. 'Hymek' class loco   F.Askey - Minolta SR3

Plate 80. Taplow Station   P.Askey - Minolta SR3

A 'Hymek' thunders past on an Up express whilst on the far right a low sided wagon is the only occupant of the head shunt and siding that ran behind the Up Relief platform. The lower picture was taken by Peter and whilst a DMU idles on the Up Relief lines Frank and daughter Shirley stroll down the centre platform. The station had just been repainted and as can be seen the original station name boards have been painted black with the letters picked out in white. Other than the repaint, the station totems and platform lighting we could have been back in the days of the Great Western.

READING APPROACHES

Plate 81. Reading South Loco & stations   5th July 1964   Minolta SR1

Plate 82. No 6991   6th September 1964   Minolta SR1

An interesting view of the south western approaches to Reading General in July 1964 complete with a full array of semaphore signals and the Southern connecting lines. Reading South, the former Southern Railway station, finally closed in September 1965 and is clearly visible behind the empty loco depot which itself closed in January of that year. Taken at approximately the same location as above but looking north 'Modified Hall' No.6991, formerly *Acton Burnell Hall*, shunts in the eastern yards with high-rise office blocks beginning to change Reading town's landscape.

Plate 83. No.7011 *Banbury Castle*   14th July 1963   Mamiya C22

Plate 84. No.4088 *Dartmouth Castle*   26th August 1962   Fed-2

'Castle' class No.7011 *Banbury Castle* is held by signals at Reading General station whilst on an Up parcels in July 1963. A Reading allocated engine she has faintly visible chalked marking '1N 36', on her smoke box, which shows she must have recently worked an express destined for the north east. Meanwhile a year earlier another 'Castle' class No.4088 *Dartmouth Castle* pauses briefly at Reading General with a full head of steam on a Paddington bound train, the fireman using the opportunity to possibly rake coal forward.

Plate 85. No.5076 *Gladiator*   30th September 1962   Fed-2

Plate 86. No.7816 *Frilsham Manor*   14th July 1963   Mamiya C22

Another 'Castle' class locomotive No.5076 *Gladiator* holds the middle running lines on the Slow, or Relief lines, at Reading General station. She would be waiting for a train up from the south to run into the station before taking the train on northwards. Meanwhile 'Manor' class No.7816 *Frilsham Manor* waits in a eastern bay platform, its locomotive lamps set for express train working, but more likely a newspaper train

Plate 87. No.7904 *Fountains Hall*   12th July 1964   Minolta SR1

Plate 88. Front Ends   14th July 1963   Mamiya C22

Photographed from our South Wales train 'Modified Hall' No.7904 *Fountains Hall*, without its front number plate, lurks over on the Down Relief side of the Reading General station. It was a Sunday so that would explain the abandoned trolleys and somewhat deserted look to the place.

One of my few impulse photographs which occurred too infrequently. The Great Western 'Manor' is stationary whilst the Southern Mogul runs through light engine. possibly to the GW loco depot. The Southern terminus is glimpsed between the locomotives.

Plate 89. No.2257   14th July 1963   Mamiya C22

Plate 90. No.7927   October 1964   Minolta SR1

'2251' class No.2257 with a ballast working stationary on the middle road between the main running lines at the eastern end of Reading General station. The picture presents a fine view of the main station buildings, semaphore signals, and even a Bedford Dormobile parked alongside the Southern Railway station. Another photograph taken as we pull out of Reading General, 'Modified Hall' No.7927, formerly *Willington Hall* heads up a LNER Gresley full van on a Down train. Note those high rise offices in the right background, somehow they just don't sit well in the picture.

Plate 91. No.6980   6th September 1964   Minolta SR1

Plate 92. Reading Loco Sheds   19th July 1964   Minolta SR1

We continue with a selection of 'through the carriage window' shots with yet another 'Modified Hall' No.6980 formerly *Llanrumney Hall* just west of Reading General station assisting with some ballast working. The 'Modified Halls' featured in the last few pictures all survived till December 1965 when the class became extinct. Taking the southern curve out of Reading on a Westbury train, Reading loco sheds come into full view with the 1932 repair shop on the right and the depot's stationary boiler on the extreme left. Five months after this photograph was taken the shed closed.

Plate 93. No.7813 *Freshford Manor*   Minolta SR1

Plate 94. No.6938 *Corndean Hall*   Minolta SR1

Two photographs taken of Reading Loco yards on 5th July 1964 from a Swindon bound train. The locomotives featured in both pictures are 'Manor' class No.7813 *Freshford Manor* in the top and 'Hall' class No.6938 *Corndean Hall* in the lower. Featuring in both pictures are the large water towers in the distance alongside the southern curve. Whilst neatly stored oil drums and old fashioned wheel barrows set a scene in the top picture, a busy one presents itself in the lower with two locomotives in steam behind our 'Hall' and a class '28xx' receiving some attention.

Plate 95. No 7337   5th July 1964   Minolta SR1

Plate 96. Goring Troughs   12th July 1964   Minolta SR!

'43xx' class No.7337 coupled to a Southern brake van shunts the extensive Reading West yards. Note the guard's pushbike, which one hopes, is securely attached. This locomotive was one of the last built, originally as No.9315, with outside steam pipes and cab windows and she was withdrawn two months after this photograph was taken. The lower picture shows that I've just managed to capture the Goring troughs before finally running over them. By the date of this picture there was little demand for them and they went out of use the following year.

DIDCOT APPROACHES - 5th JULY 1964

Plate 97. No.2248   Minolta SR1

Plate 98. No.6136   Minolta SR1

Running near to Didcot '2251'class No.2248 wheezes away on a ballast train. She has two months left in service and already looks in a bad way with boiler cladding adrift, painted smoke box number, and lacking cab plates. Her GW 'Toad' brake van seems to have wandered off its territory somewhat, being restricted to Coleham (Salop). I suppose the ganger's white shirt would pass for 1960s high-viz jacket then. The young fireman on a more presentable '61xx' class No.6136 is, I fancy, under test as a close up shows a possible inspector with collar and tie in the background.

Plate 99. No.D7027   30th September 1962   Fed-2

Plate 100. No.6983 *Otterington Hall*   19th July 1964   Minolta SR1

Last of the 'through the carriage window' views with an unspectacular attempt of catching 'Hymek' class diesel No.D7027 on a Paddington bound train comprised of LMS stock. Other than getting everything in the way of our train engine you might say the picture is a success, good shot of the telegraph poles though. Two years later 'Modified Hall' No.6983 *Otterington Hall* shunts an LMS parcels van in Didcot yards alongside the railway station with, in the distance, the transfer shed which would find preservation years later at the Didcot Railway Centre.

Plate 101. No.1007   30th September 1962   Fed-2

Plate 102. Nos.D6527 & D6556   19th July 1964   Minolta SR1

Deep in Didcot's carriage sidings the driver of 'County' class No.1007 *County of Brecknock* seems to be awaiting the signal to either pull off or couple up for one of the locomotive's last duties. She has a tender full of coal but with nameplates removed she was days away from withdrawal. Taken up at the throat of Didcot's loco shed yards, two Crompton diesels Nos.D6527 & D6556 quietly hum away to themselves having just come in. Although only a year or so old No.D6527 has already sustained some near-side crash damage.

Plate 103. No.5016 *Montgomery Castle*   26th August 1962   Fed-2

Plate 104. No.6995 *Benthall Hall*   5th July 1964   Minolta SR1

On a Sunday visit to Swindon Works I just caught 'Castle' class No.5016 *Montgomery Castle* on a Bristol train with the spire of St. Marks church in the background. This must have been one of her last duties as withdrawal came within weeks. Meanwhile, some two years later following a Swindon Works visit and so off to Gloucester, I just caught 'Modified Hall' No.6995 *Benthall Hall* running light engine to the loco sheds.

Plate 105. Locomotives awaiting scrap   Minolta SR1

Plate 106. Locomotives awaiting scrap   Minolta SR1

Two photographs taken on 12th July 1964 whilst passing Swindon Works on a trip to South Wales. Both pictures show withdrawn locomotives waiting scrapping. The top picture shows the boiler and erecting shops in the background with what looks to be an LMS loco and tender with Nos.1451, 1627 and 9450 for scrap. Moving along somewhat Nos.8743, 7436 and 2818 feature outside the corner of the iron foundry with the large water tank mounted above the pattern shop. All the locos were scrapped by the following month save No.2818 which survived the cutter's torch.

Plate 107. Loco Shed and coaling plant   31st. January 1965   Minolta SR1

Plates 108. Fuelling depot and Station
August 1971   Halina 35mm

By January 1965 Swindon motive power depot was in serious decline and the deserted coaling plant looks to be derelict. It would be doubtful whether the two locomotives would be going anywhere, however the picture gives some notion to the size of the depot. The two small lower pictures are somewhat out of time in this book, both taken in August 1971. The top view illustrates the demise of part of the old GW platform buildings and footbridge whilst the lower gives some idea of the reduction in motive power Swindon now being little more than a stabling point.

BERKS & HANTS AND WESTBURY YARDS

Plates 109.   Views from a train   6th September 1964   Minolta SR1

Plate 110. No.4569   19th July 1964   Minolta SR1

Plate 109 comprises two photographs taken on 6th September 1964 from an Exeter bound train somewhere on the Berks & Hants line. For me an odd thing to do but I thought I would include them. Our train engine is a 'Warship' class diesel whilst in the lower picture a '28xx' appears to be on a ballast train. Good shots of telegraph poles again. Plate 110 has a '45xx' tank, No.4569, paused from shunting duties in the yards opposite Westbury locomotive depot, whilst the 'Hymek' is in charge of a mixed bag of wagons including a Southern utility van.

ASKEY FAMILY HOLIDAYS - 1960

Plate 111. Nos.6836 *Estevarney Grange* & 7009 *Athelny Castle*   August 1960   F.Askey - Kershaw

Plate 112. No.4920 *Dumbleton Hall*   August 1960   F.Askey - Kershaw

Peter Askey's family, like most people of the time, had one weeks annual holiday. So it was that 13-year-old Peter went to Cornwall in August 1960. Even at this stage diesels were making heavy inroads into steam workings so Frank, Peter's dad, caught steam's last gasp. The two pictures shown are No.6836 *Estevarney Grange* and No.7009 *Athelny Castle* double heading out of Newton Abbot with a Penzance train, whilst the lower picture has 'Hall' class No.4920 *Dumbleton Hall* on a Down goods passing Totnes station and Brunel's never used atmospheric engine house.

ASKEY FAMILY HOLIDAYS - 1960

Plate 113. No.5003 *Lulworth Castle*   August 1960   F.Askey - Kershaw

Plate 114. No.1018 *County of Leicester*   August 1960   F.Askey - Kershaw

Paignton's gas works was railway connected and even owned its own diesel shunter, and forms a backdrop to these two pictures. 'Castle' class No.5003 *Lulworth Castle* is possibly on a Down empty carriage stock working caught from the road bridge, whilst 'County' class No.1018 *County of Leicester* is photographed just along the line on a stopping train. Inconsiderate of the driver of the little Austin, he could have driven up a second or so later. These pictures mean much to me, I remember being in Frank's darkened kitchen under the glow of the red safety light watching the images appear in developing tray.

Plate 115. North British Type 2 & No.4564   F.Askey - Kershaw

Plate 116. 'Warship' class   F.Askey - Kershaw

Two more pictures from the Askey family holiday, Cornwall again but it's 1961 . . . and diesels.
On reflection Cornwall in the 1960s was England's holiday paradise. Even in those days cars would queue for hours on the A30 Honiton by pass. The BBC would take to the air to film the never ending jams. Meanwhile our top picture has a unidentified North British diesel hydraulic double heading with '45xx' class loco No.4564 pulling out of St. Ives. A fitting end, Penzance sea wall and station form a backdrop to another unidentified diesel, this time a 'Warship' in original condition.

Plate 117. No.7019 *Fowey Castle*   June 1963   Mamiya C22

Plate 118. No.3620   June 1963   Mamiya C22

Old Oak Common formed the junction of the Bristol and Birmingham main lines. Looking north up the Birmingham line towards North Acton 'Castle' class No.7019 *Fowey Castle* is working an Up express train into Paddington. At this stage, June 1963, it is either an excursion or substitute for a failed diesel. Looking in the opposite direction towards London, with Old Oak's carriage sidings in the background, '57xx' pannier class No.3620 is working a local stopping goods, possibly up to Park Royal or Greenford.

Inset. No.6963's Engine Crew

Plate 119. No.6963 *Throwley Hall* 26th July 1963 Mamiya C22

Plate 120. 'Castle' class loco c.1962 P.Wells - Kodak 44A

Taken from Coronation Road footbridge at Park Royal, 'Modified Hall' class No.6963 *Throwley Hall* has pulled off the Birmingham main line prior to taking its short train either up to the local goods yard or possibly the Guinness factory. The inset picture shows the only occasion on which I photographed an engine crew. Meanwhile, in the lower picture, Paul Wells has caught an unidentified 'Castle' working a Down train at speed somewhere near to Hanger Lane. This panned shot, admittedly the best of several, is more than creditable as taken with a Kodak 44A box camera.

Plate 121. No.D1700   25th July 1964   Minolta SR1

Inset: Greenford Station LT & BR   Late 1964

Plate 122. No.5098 *Clifford Castle*   September 1963   P.Askey - Minolta A5

A Sulzer diesel waits on the Up platform at the British Railways station of Greenford as seen looking west from the higher level LT station. The Down platform buildings are replacements for the original ones demolished in the 1940s to make way for the LT extension. Both the inset and lower picture are of the 4.15pm Bicester out of Paddington. The inset picture catches the Ealing Broadway DMU service in the bay with an eastbound Underground train, and in the far right distance the cupola stacks of the British Bath Works - and that's me hanging out of the carriage window.

GREENFORD - MY HOME TOWN

Teddy was born in 1945 at Hammersmith Hospital, West London, which had the Great Western Railway running past its front door and the GW main running lines over the back. Old Oak Common loco sheds were less than a mile away so I must have had the smell of them. Ideal credentials for a trainspotter. Next door was Wormwood Scrubs prison. Have so far evaded such establishments. So I was off to a good start.

Just to confuse people the hospital wasn't actually in Hammersmith but we made up for it by living there. The family moved to Greenford Green, Middlesex in 1948 which was situated north of Greenford town and the former Great Western railway line. By 1954 we had moved again into Greenford proper, south of the railway and an easy walk to the station. As young children we would play on the local dump or would sneak up near to Greenford station and place pennies on the railway tracks to wait for passing express trains to do their worse. We would wait and wait and wait. As a prelude to trainspotting this told us that Ealing or Southall on Paddington's 'other' main line was a better bet. Greenford would be my home till I was twenty five, I was, for all intents and purposes, a West London lad and 1930s suburbia was my home. It was one of open spaces, housing, and manufacturing industries. And it was busy. On weekdays the world went to work and the roads would be crammed with workers of all ilks walking, cycling or travelling by motorbike, car or bus. In the early 1960s the car was still in its infancy and unaffordable for most working people. Greenford's suburban streets were mostly devoid of the parked car. On Saturday nights the pubs were full as were the picture palaces and the dance halls. Sunday was still the Sabbath so on Sunday you rested. Sunday was dead. For us young men, motorbikes were our day-to-day transport and for those older and married the three wheeler combination would suffice. But for those who cared to look there was still an old Greenford which pre-dated the suburbia which had all but drowned it. There were even Greenford folk born and bred in a previous era that spoke with a country-like accent. Marriage moved me out of the area in 1970 and redundancy five years later virtually broke all ties with my old town. However, as you can see there's a bit of Greenford in me. And as this particular book has taken me into nostalgia land perhaps you can cope with a bit of social history and industrial heritage before returning to the plot.

Without doing a 'Timeteam' on you, let it be said that back in 1901 Greenford's population numbered around 650. Other than a few large country houses for the gentry, agriculture was the mainstay of the area. The arrival of the Grand Junction canal, later to become the Grand Union canal in 1800 was the first major transport link serving both agriculture and, eventually, industry. The canal also brought rubbish, tons of the stuff from London, which was tipped at Greenford near to where the A40 Western Avenue would eventually cross. Tipping refuse ceased just prior to the Second World War and by my time this area had become known as 'The Dump'. Despite becoming heavily overgrown and with warnings of contaminated land, this was our playground and hours would be spent hunting down all manner of snakes, from the humble slowworm to the poisonous adder.

Brickmaking was the first Industry that came to Greenford area but the establishment of Perkins dye works in 1857 along the canal at Greenford Green put the area on the map. It rapidly expanded and became a large concern. The chemical processes were extremely hazardous and following several serious accidents the company was sold off and by 1880 had gone with some of the buildings being put to other uses. However it has been said that Greenford was the birthplace of the modern organic dye industry. By 1904 the Great Western Railway had opened a station at Greenford on its new line which connected Paddington to High Wycombe and onwards to Birmingham. The coming of the railway opened up

Greenford station Up side buildings in the late Edwardian era.
(Courtesy Frances and Peter Hounsell)

industrial concerns to the east of Greenford station between the railway and the canal. These initial companies were Baileys glass works and Purex Ltd a lead paint manufacturer whose processes became more deadly than the dye works. The Great War came to Greenford with the opening of

a large rail connected munitions plant. This was situated just along from the glass works and was in actual fact a shell filling station for the assembling of lethal, i.e. chemical, shells. Such was the demand for shells during the war that many of these filling stations were opened around the country. Sadly, accidents occasionally occurred resulting in tragic loss of life. After the war the whole site was taken up by the Rockware Glass Syndicate, a major bottle producer. Covering some 35 acres its railway sidings, furnaces, and tall chimney feature as a backdrop in several of the photographs in this book.

The former shell filling buildings with Rockware Glass in the background. *(Courtesy London Borough of Ealing)*

In the early post war years further industry was attracted to the area and by 1921 the J. Lyons tea and food company had opened their factory just to the north west of Greenford station. With extensive railway sidings and its own locomotives the factory also had its own canal dock basin. By the early 1930s some 14,000 people were employed there and this figure was to double again by the 1950s with the opening of an ice cream plant built opposite the original factory on the northern bank of the Grand Union canal.

South west of Greenford station opposite the Lyons factory the British Bath Works opened their foundry and enamelling plant in 1928. This was rail connected off a long spur which eventually ran down to the Kelvin construction company and terminated at Aladdins, an American lamp and heater concern which opened its factory in 1931. Road improvements were under way by the mid 1930s the main arterial road, the Western Avenue, ran through Greenford south of the railway with the imposing Aladdin building situated alongside. Hopes that new factories would open up along the Western Avenue at Greenford were dashed and the Aladdin factory was to remain in isolation. The last major company to move in to the area in the inter-war years was Glaxo Laboratories which opened in 1935 at Greenford Green. Although not rail connected it was located alongside the northern bank of the Grand Union canal and barges would supply the company with coal. An overhead crane system would transfer the coal from barge to the rear of the factory and as a child I would sit and watch the chain and grab scooping

Allied Ironfounders, British Bath Works c.1960. *(Courtesy London Borough of Ealing)*

The Alladin building alongside Western Avenue c.1960. *(Courtesy London Borough of Ealing)*

up coal from barges moored alongside the canal bank.

The last major construction undertaken in this period was a large Central Ordnance Depot for the Royal Army Ordnance Corps built just prior to the Second World War. This was located between the Aladdin factory and the British Bath Works and was a sub-depot to the Woolwich Arsenal. It comprised of some twenty buildings responsible for the distribution of military stores worldwide. At its peak around 3000 civilian and military personnel were employed with Nissen hutted accommodation camps spread around the immediate area. It could be said that Greenford during the Second World War would have been really humming. Taking into account the RAOC depot and all of the factories it was a far cry from six hundred odd people some forty years previous.

As children growing up in the 1950s our schooling did not do war, well not the Second World War. Our history lessons ceased when things started to get interesting. We found war exciting, several of our teachers had been through it and could be coaxed into telling us about it . . . better than lessons anyway. Our maths teacher went through the desert with Monty, he could tell a good story especially about being lost in the desert. "Please sir, please sir, did you drink your own urine sir . . .?".

Parents said little, especially the women. No death or glory there. There was little in Greenford to relate to, parents would occasionally drag you round London for shopping which revealed many bombsites. Trips out with Buster around the south London loco sheds produced even more bombsites, some areas still razed to the ground. And then there were prefabs of course. Just on the outskirts of Greenford there was a pub sign with no pub. Called 'The Load of Hay'. We often played there but of a pub there was no sign. Children died there, the pub receiving a direct hit during September 1940 killing everyone. The following day the Medway Estate, east of Greenford station, took a hit from a land mine, again, with tragic loss of life. A few weeks later the Luftwaffe became personal for my wife's family. With a bomb going between the air raid shelters and finally exploding under a service road a rather dazed Vic, Iris's dad, emerged to fall into the bomb crater. Throughout 1940 and the next few years Greenford took sporadic hits including the Lyons factory, housing, parks and fields etc.

Towards the end of hostilities the V1, doodle bug, made its presence felt with three hits, one directly on Glaxos, fortunately with no loss of life. Sadly in March 1945, with the last V1s being launched, one of the Army Ordnance buildings suffered a direct hit with terrible loss of life.

Greenford's war seemed to start and finish with tragedy.

Following the war no other major manufactures came to Greenford but there was a host of smaller concerns. Work was plentiful; the factories were busy and commercial traffic on the roads was heavy.

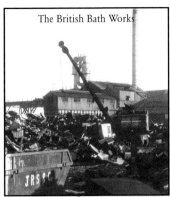
The British Bath Works

Scrap

Charging

Melting Plant

Bath Casting

Lorries rumbled around at 25mph as did most London Transport double decker RTs and RTLs, but I don't remember seeing the new RM Routemaster buses. What was novel were bus and lorry chassis being driven around on test from the nearby giant AEC factory at Southall. These were monstrous machines with open engines and a driver strapped into his seat with no protection whatsoever other than an old sack over his legs to protect him from the elements. With goggles and a cap he resembled a First World War fighter pilot. Late at night you could hear heavy freight trains slogging through Greenford station and shunting going on in the railway yards nearby. Rainy days would bring a change of air traffic approach to London Airport and the sky would resonate to Vickers Viscounts, Britannias, Constellations, Stratocruisers and Comets. Plane spotting was considered but required good eyesight and binoculars, I had neither. So that ruled that out on both counts. On still nights shunting up at the railway yards would become background sounds as the ton up lads on big British singles and twins would throttle off and then accelerate away from the many roundabouts on the Western Avenue till they faded away on the long straight past Northolt airport.

When Bob Keelers Ltd, Greenford's own motor bike dealers, paraded the new Japanese 250cc Honda Dreams with pressed steel chassis and square front headlamps on the pavement outside the shop they were met with ridicule and contempt. Feelings still ran strong in some quarters over this, seeing Japanese products including cameras on display with the last war only finishing some fifteen years previous.

After initially starting work at Qualcast foundry, Ealing, I eventually commenced an apprenticeship in 1963 as a metallurgical chemist at Allied Ironfounders, British Bath Works. This was not good news in some quarters as the company had a terrible local reputation. It was regarded as being a dirty noisy horrible place emitting all manner of smoke and smuts, and that was just the factory let alone those who worked there. However I was to find the factory staff amongst the friendliest folk I ever met, though the office staff could be somewhat snooty. But that's the way it was then. Although based in the laboratory you would soon find yourself working down in the foundry and mainly on the melting plant. This comprised of two cupolas, or furnaces, whose stacks reached some seventy feet high and ran molten iron into giant receivers at around six tons an hour. Telphers, connected to overhead track, would take the molten cast iron in ladles to the several bath moulding plants. To do this, with flashing lights and with alarms ringing in your ears, they would run onto an overhead traverser to change tracks and God help you if the telpher ladle had been overfilled. The noise from these and the moulding machines and the filth is difficult to explain if you have never worked in such an environment. Outside the foundry the cupolas

Ted at British Bath Works melting plant area, 1964.

Ted at British Bath Works laboratories, printing pictures of sprint motorcycles!

would be fed with scrap iron, limestone and coke in huge quantities from an overhead crane which ran along its own towering gantry. Although the metal scrap and limestone came by road the coke was delivered by train which ran under the gantry courtesy of a pannier tank or, in later years, a diesel shunter. On a few occasions if labour was short you had to fork out coke from the wagons yourself, now that's what you call 'hands on' railway experience. On one occasion when us apprentices were up in arms over work we thought not to be quite 'us' the managing director, Mr George Webster, sent down a red lined Internal Memo to all departmental managers. I quote. APPRENTICES MUST NOT LABOUR, BUT ARE EXPECTED TO PULL THEIR WEIGHT. No answer to that then.

The Bath Works site stretched back as far as the Grand Union canal. In my day there were many railway sidings, red raw with rust, at the rear of the works that I believe possibly ran into the former RAOC site. By this time the central ordinance depot had long gone and the site had become an industrial estate. Around our sidings were mountains of scrap iron comprised of anything that local scrap merchants could get into a skip or fit on a lorry. The most recognisable things were old style large radiators, car and bike engines, gearboxes, and more sewing machines than you could throw a stick at. Railway chairs would not be accepted as of poor quality, the occasional railway sign or veteran motor cycle engine, when found, was liberated by myself even to the point of stopping the cupola charge bucket.

Greenford station when built back in 1904 was, for the area at that time, quite substantial being brick built throughout and having through loop lines off the central running tracks. These and the station were on a grass embankment and inclined approach roads gave access to the station buildings, flights of stairs running up to platform level. A lift was available for luggage etc. Throughout the 1920s and '30s suburbia and factories spread along the railway and the station acquired its own local pub, naturally named 'The Railway'. In the 1960s the pub sign was an excellent painting of, for a pub sign that is, a Great Western 'King'. Sadly some time later this was changed for, can you believe it, a 'Warship' diesel.

The biggest change to the railway at Greenford came in the 1930s when traffic demands required an extension of the London Passenger Transport Board Central Line westwards from North Acton. The Central Line electrified tracks would run parallel to the Down Great Western main line and the existing stations and halts would be replaced by new LPTB ones. Work started in the late 1930s but was halted during the Second World War with construction recommencing thereafter. The new Greenford station was situated slightly to the east of the GW station and finally opened in 1947 with the final extension to West Ruislip the following year. This resulted in radical changes at Greenford. To give access for the Central Line tracks they had to be elevated at a level considerably higher than the Great Western. Large bridges, viaducts and embankments had to be constructed over the Greenford to Ealing loop line and the sidings to Aladdin and British Bath Works. This was achieved by a massive structure built alongside the GW running lines and a new station

The new Greenford station opened in 1947, seen in mid-1960s.
(Courtesy London Transport Museum)

entrance at ground level with a subway connecting it to the original station. The Central Lines were split by an island platform with a middle bay to give access to Great Western trains running in at a steep incline from the Greenford loop serving Ealing. The old station would suffer further humiliation having to have its Great Western Down station buildings demolished to allow for the new Underground Central Line tracks. They were replaced by a simple brick built waiting room. On the opening of the Central Line the old station lost its passenger workings and, despite remaining open for parcel traffic and occasional excursion work,

Greenford station mid-1950s with the Ealing Broadway auto-train service.
(Courtesy Dewi Williams)

finally closed in 1963. The main line remained busy with 'King' and 'Castle' hauled Birmingham and Chester trains till replaced by diesels hydraulics during 1962 and then Sulzer diesel electrics in 1964. The part closure and electrification of the Euston line kept the line busy, but with the opening of the Euston to Birmingham service in 1967 the Paddington service was rapidly discontinued.

Local freight workings dwindled away from the 1960s onwards and of the manufacturing factories that came to Greenford in the inter-war years Rockware Glass was the first to go in 1973. The British Bath Works closed in 1975 and Aladdins went at about the same time. Through the 1990s the Lyons empire had broken up and its various product lines sold off and moved out leaving only Glaxo Laboratories. Sadly by 2010 even they had gone.

But Greenford's Great Western railway station will remain with us forever, captured on film in the very first and last episodes of 'The Likely Lads' shown during 1964/65. The first episode shows the Down platform with the London Transport Central Line running across in the background, a quick glimpse of Greenford West signal box and the spur line running off under the LT tracks to the British Bath Works with its towering cupola stacks. In the last episode our heroes Bob and Terry meet up outside the Up side station buildings, Terry having volunteered for the army to join Bob with poor Bob being rejected for having flat feet. A long lingering shot shows Terry being driven off in a army truck going up the approach road towards the goods yard.

Greenford Revisited

Greenford 2010 is not the place of my youth. As far as the railway goes the 'Kings', 'Castles', 'Westerns' and Sulzers have long gone. The old Great Western line from Paddington to the Midlands that ran through Greenford is now reduced to a rusty single track almost covered by undergrowth, the station cut back to platform levels and what buildings remain covered in graffiti. Good material for a 'Now and Then' book, but not here.

Modern for its time the 1930s dual carriageway Western Avenue that ran through Greenford with its spacious roundabouts, period pubs and roadside garages have given way to an expressway with flyovers and underpasses. It's now simply the A40.

The Greenford that I took for granted in the 1950s which would have been a blot on the landscape to an older generation has in my turn gone to be replaced by warehousing. Clean, tidy, and presentable . . .

Strangely whilst the fortunes of rail and road have changed completely the canal remains the same, untouched by the modern world.

The Aladdin building, just along from the canal, remains as isolated as ever on the A40. After closure the buildings eventually became a 'Do it Yourself' outlet but when this moved out the building now stands empty and the site boarded up. The RAOC site which stretched from Aladdins to the British Bath Works is now a gated trading estate and the Bath Works has become the Fairway Trading Estate. Of the long siding that ran down to Aladdins the trackbed is discernable along the old Bath Works site, but of the Bath Works there is no trace. The late 1940s replacement station is as busy as ever serving both London Transport and the Network Rail spur to Ealing Broadway. North of the railway the Lyons empire has totally gone its grand entrance of white pillars and large iron gates, poplar trees and factories having been replaced by modern warehousing. The Rockware site is now occupied by IBM, the Royal Mail and a giant retail park whilst up at Greenford Green the pharmaceutical concern of Glaxo Laboratories with its art deco style offices remain but its future is unknown.

Most of our old drinking haunts still survive in one form or another except the Oldfield and its dancehall, where I met Iris . . . it's a block of flats.

Above: The old Lyons factory main gates in 2003, photographed shortly before demolition. *(Courtesy Funky Anorak)*

Opposite page top: A Lyons company publicity photograph c.1939. Of interest on the top right hand corner is the Grand Union canal with dock basin (see also top inset) and crossing the top of the photograph diagonally is the Great Western main line with newly installed earthworks and bridge for the future LTPB extension prior to the laying of tracks. Top middle can be seen part of the gantry of British Bath Works where approximately 25 years later I took many of the photographs that appear over the following pages. *(Courtesy City of London, London Metropolitan Archives)*

Opposite page bottom: Photograph of Greenford Green, 1947, showing in the foreground the pharmaceutical concern of Glaxo Laboratories and the Lyons confectionery factory immediately behind and to the left. The Grand Union canal threads its way through the centre of the photograph. Take note in front of the canal bridge is the facility for unloading coal from barges using an overhead gantry. The Great Western running lines cross the top of the photograph with the British Bath Works immediately behind. The lower inset shows the Glaxo factory following the V1 attack in August 1944. *(Courtesy GlaxoSmithKline group of companies)*

Plate 123. No.6027 *King Richard I*   Fed-2

Plate 124. No.6025 *King Henry III*   Fed-2

Greenford station was on the former Great Western main line to the Midlands and the North West. 'King' class locomotives were regular performers on this, their last regular service. Their final swansong came at the end of 1962. With, at best, an hourly service and sometimes not a lot of train movements between this line was never a trainspotter's first choice. The two pictures, both taken in August 1962, depict No.6027 *King Richard I* on a Midlands bound express whilst the lower picture has No.6025 *King Henry III* still with a plentiful supply of coal running on into Paddington.

Plate 125. No.5038 *Morlais Castle*   26th June 1963   Mamiya C22

Plate 126. No.7008 *Swansea Castle*   25th July 1963   Maimya C22

The GW Midlands main line would host the last regular steam working out of Paddington, the 4.15pm to Bicester, calling at Gerrards Cross, High Wycombe, and Princess Risborough. The train normally consisted of four coaches and a parcels van. The two 1963 pictures have 'Castles' No.5038 *Morlais Castle* running through the station whilst No.7008 *Swansea Castle* is still a short distance away. Greenford's semaphore signals form the background in this picture whilst a London bound underground train waits at the later build London Transport station.

Plate 127. No.6999 *Capel Dewi Hall*   June 1964   Minolta SR1

Plate 128. No.6812 *Chesford Grange*   29th July 1963   Mamiya C22

Another shot of the 4.15pm to Bicester with 'Modified Hall' No.6999 *Capel Dewi Hall* taken in June 1964. Twelve months later steam bowed out on this service and that was that as far as Paddington was concerned. 'Grange' class locomotives were not too common so it was a surprise to see No.6812 *Chesford Grange* ambling along on a short Up through goods. Sadly I suppose the large wooden 'passengers' sign eventually went to the bonfire after closure. I always positioned myself on the 'modernised' Down platform as I considered the GW buildings aesthetically a better alternative.

Plate 129. No.6135   27th August 1963   Mamiya C22

Plate 130. No.9420   27th April 1963   Mamiya C22

An interesting and lucky photograph of the Inspector's coach in chocolate brown and cream livery being pulled by '61xx' class No.6135 on the through Up lines. Greenford is still busy with parcel traffic, note the Southern van in the bay platform with the Lyons factory in the background. The lower picture, and the following two, show the day-to-day life around Greenford station, panniers shunting and working local goods. '94xx' class No.9420 pulls through on the Up loop with a container train

GREENFORD STATION

Plate 131. No.8768   26th June 1963   Mamiya C22

Plate 132. No.9710   27th June 1963   Mamiya C22

Whilst waiting for the 4.15pm Bicester train on two consecutive days in June 1963 I caught goods trains being worked up at the Greenford Lyons factory. In the top picture '57xx' class No.8768 has pulled up alongside the Up platform whilst condensing tank No.9710 is shunting the yards. Lyons were involved in cyclic goods movements, trains loaded with tea worked overnight from Greenford down to Bristol via Acton with a return Up overnight working of chocolate from Fry's factories at Keynsham and Somerdale. This Up working was known as the 'The Cocoa'. Reminds me of Henry the Green Engine and the 'Flying Kipper'.

Plate 133. No.61087   20th July 1963   Mamiya C22

Plate 134. No.61138   17th August 1963   Mamiya C22

Being more of a trainspotter than a railway photographer only number, date, and location were recorded. The following four pictures are Saturday inter-regional trains, and for me to be at Greenford station I must have had prior knowledge of these workings. Of the two former LNER class 'B1s' No.61087 is hauling LMS stock whilst with No.61138 the leading coaches are of LNER origin, the first coach being a Gresley with possibly a Thompson backing it up. These locomotives would work light engine through Greenford some hours earlier, possibly working these trains back from Kensington Olympia.

Plate 135. No.44691   22nd June 1963   Mamiya C22

Plate 136. No.45417   17th August 1963   Mamiya C22

Two LMS 'Black 5s' photographed slightly to the east of Greenford station with the Rockware Glass Works as a backdrop. Unlike the previous pictures these have paper train reporting numbers and whilst the destination of No.44691 in the top picture is somewhere on the Midland region No.45417 could possibly a charter train working. Again we seem to have a mix of coaching stock, a Mk I brake, possibly a LNER coach and a rake of LMS stock. However it has to be remembered that in the 1960s the oldest coaching stock going finished up on excursion train workings.

Plate 137. No.48007   27th June 1963   Mamiya C22

Plate 138. No.48727   29th July 1963   Mamiya C22

During weekdays there could, on occasions, be considerable goods workings. LMS locomotives were not uncommon and these two class '8Fs' would, again, be photographed in the late afternoon whilst waiting for the 4.15pm Bicester train. No.48007 is on an Up through goods and directly behind the locomotive stands the goods yard water column and on the far right vans can be seen in Lyon's own sidings. Another Up working has No.48727 fitted with a Fowler tender. She was an interesting loco, built at Brighton in 1944 and allocated to the LNER till transferred to the LMS in 1947.

Plate 139. No.90697   19th May 1963   Mamiya C22

Plate 140. Sulzer Type 2   August 1964   Minolta SR1

Like all railway lines you get the not so common and these two pictures show locomotive classes not seen very often by myself. 'War Department' 2-8-0 No.90697 heads an Up through freight. At one time fairly common at Southall loco shed I do not recall seeing 'WDs' "clink clanking" their way through Greenford very often. The "clink clank" refers to the loco's motion, you wouldn't want your car engine to sound like it. The unidentified Type 2 Sulzer is an unusual class on this route working an Eastern Region bound express, somewhat underpowered one only hopes it managed arrive on time.

DIESEL ELECTRICS AT GREENFORD - 1964

Plate 141. No. D1723   July 1964   Minolta SR1

Plate 142. No.D1694   August 1964   Minolta SR1

By 1963 all Midlands bound trains were in the hands of 'Western' class diesel hydraulics but by early 1964 they had been replaced by Type 4 Sulzers. Both pictures date from the summer of 1964 and these workings has been transferred to the Midland Region. Down trains show 'M' for a Midland Region destination whilst 'V' would be trains coming from the north on to the Western Region. The trackbed through Greenford is a credit to the men working the line knowing that within a few years it would be downgraded. In the left distance is Greenford West signal box and the line leading off to The British Bath Works.

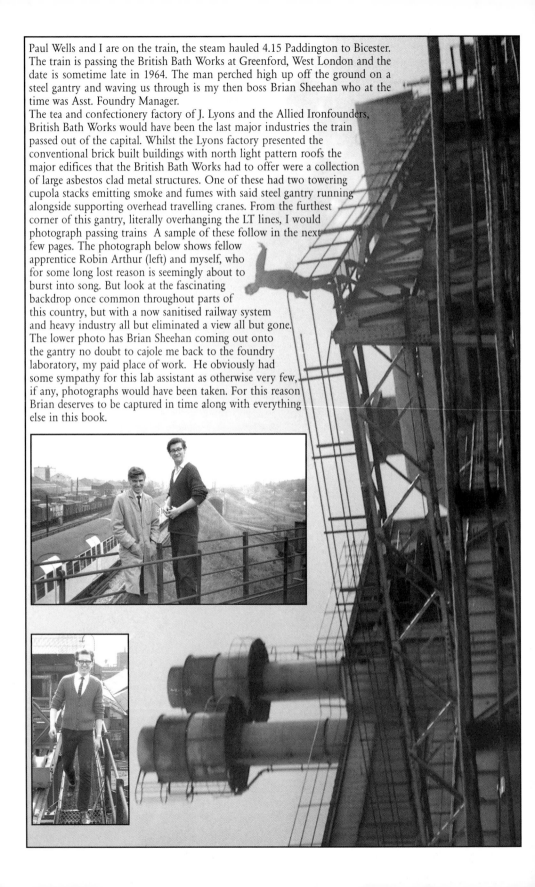

Paul Wells and I are on the train, the steam hauled 4.15 Paddington to Bicester. The train is passing the British Bath Works at Greenford, West London and the date is sometime late in 1964. The man perched high up off the ground on a steel gantry and waving us through is my then boss Brian Sheehan who at the time was Asst. Foundry Manager.

The tea and confectionery factory of J. Lyons and the Allied Ironfounders, British Bath Works would have been the last major industries the train passed out of the capital. Whilst the Lyons factory presented the conventional brick built buildings with north light pattern roofs the major edifices that the British Bath Works had to offer were a collection of large asbestos clad metal structures. One of these had two towering cupola stacks emitting smoke and fumes with said steel gantry running alongside supporting overhead travelling cranes. From the furthest corner of this gantry, literally overhanging the LT lines, I would photograph passing trains A sample of these follow in the next few pages. The photograph below shows fellow apprentice Robin Arthur (left) and myself, who for some long lost reason is seemingly about to burst into song. But look at the fascinating backdrop once common throughout parts of this country, but with a now sanitised railway system and heavy industry all but eliminated a view all but gone. The lower photo has Brian Sheehan coming out onto the gantry no doubt to cajole me back to the foundry laboratory, my paid place of work. He obviously had some sympathy for this lab assistant as otherwise very few, if any, photographs would have been taken. For this reason Brian deserves to be captured in time along with everything else in this book.

Plate 143. No.1010 *County of Caernarvon*   1st. July 1964   Minolta SR1

Plate 144. No.3665   22nd June 1963   Mamiya C22

The British Bath Works crane gantry would seem a good vantage point for photographing trains. It certainly was for Up trains, but not quite so good coming the other way. The London Transport extension through Greenford ruined that by having to take their new tracks considerably higher than those of the old GW. By 1963 steam was restricted to excursion work and the 4.15pm Bicester service. 'County' class locos were not uncommon as No.1010 *County of Caenarvon* shows, while '57xx' class No.3665 runs past on a local goods train. Note the old sold off Lyons tea containers.

Plate 145. No.2862   15th July 1963   Mamiya C22

Plate 146. No.4954 *Plaish Hall*   22nd June 1963   Mamiya C22

  I have broken my own golden rule on this page to never repeat the same view twice in succession . . . and that's what I've done. It does show how fickle the British weather is, even in summertime, with '28xx' class No.2862 on a dull miserable day whilst the crew of 'Hall' class No.4954 *Plaish Hall* have a better day for it. Both locos are on Up goods trains and these were easier to photograph simply because the Up signal could be seen from the foundry laboratory windows. That gave me time to escape through the sand lab window and up onto the gantry . . .

Plate 147. 'Hall' class loco   July 1964   Minolta SR1

Plate 148. No.6133   28th June 1963   Minolta SR1

A unidentified 'Hall' runs through on a Down train, possibly an excursion. No exact date other than a Saturday in July so it would be morning overtime at work. Of some interest are the masts of the RAF radio station in the far background. The Luftwaffe tried to bomb them in 1940 . . . but missed hitting some of the housing in the near background instead. So that was a waste of time then. Running light '61xx' No.6133 rolls past Greenford's goods yard and the Lyons factory. We seem to have some variety of stock, a few flat trucks, vans, open and cement wagons.

GREENFORD - PASSING THE BRITISH BATH WORKS

Plate 149. No.5076 *Gladiator*   July 1963   Mamiya C22

Plate 150. No.5089 *Westminster Abbey*   20th July 1963   Mamiya C22

Sadly I didn't take many photographs looking east towards Greenford station because the London Transport tracks came down at a steep angle and obscured the BR tracks. However 'Castle' class No.5076 *Gladiator*, makes a interesting photograph with the goods yard and the Lyons factory in the background. Note the vans with tarpaulin covers over their roofs. This and the lower picture of another 'Castle' No.5089 *Westminster Abbey* are both on the 4.15pm to Bicester. Both tenders are well coaled up and again note the container train in Greenford yard's long head shunt.

Plate 151. No.7013 *Bristol Castle*　　　　　16th June 1964　　　　　Minolta SR1

Plate 152. 'Castle' class loco　　　　　June 1964　　　　　Minolta SR1

Another Saturday excursion, destination unknown, with 'Castle' class No.7013 *Bristol Castle* up front. The small scrap yard was at the far end of Greenford's yards, close up by the Grand Union Canal. I wonder if the Fordson lorry is still with us, one thing for sure the lightweight motorcycle in the scrap heap definitely isn't. It probably finished up in our cupolas in a day or so. Catching BR and LT trains passing each other rarely occurred, and on this occasion I failed to definitely catch the loco number but I think it was No.7029 *Clun Castle*. The leading coach is a GW Hawksworth.

Plate 153. 'Castle' class loco   June 1964   Minolta SR1

Plate 154. No.6803 *Bucklebury Grange*   15th June 1964   Minolta SR1

The top photograph was taken further back on the foundry lab roof and shows the original former GWR and latter day LT girder bridges crossing the Grand Union Canal. The wagons in our sidings have delivered coke and not the scrap iron alongside. The 'Castle' working a Down train is unknown but the Up mixed goods is interestingly hauled by a 'Grange', No.6803 *Bucklebury Grange*, a class not so common on this stretch of line.

Plate 155. No.7929 *Wyke Hall*   24th August 1963   Mamiya C22

Plate 156. 'Modified Hall' class loco   29th July 1963   Mamiya C22

'Modified Hall' No.7929 *Wyle Hall* pulls her train of maroon Mk I carriages, some might say 'posh' stock for a Saturday excursion. One more photograph from the foundry lab roof, an unidentified 'Hall' trundles past with a train of empty wagons. The foundry labs were responsible for chemical analysis of cast iron and moulding sand quality and it was expected of you to do some work, not spend the day train spotting. From the lab windows you could not see the trains due to the concrete-faced railway embankment, only the signals, so you never knew what you had missed. Sadly many trains just sailed past.

Plate 157. No.D1707   4th July 1964   Minolta SR1

Plate 158. No.D1689   4th July 1964   Minolta SR1

My trips out of the lab window and up to the crane gantry only lasted for just over a year. Starting my apprenticeship in June 1963 regular steam working was nearly up and the 'Western' hydraulics were soon gone. Whilst I suspect the management turned a blind eye to my antics you couldn't push your luck, although my high level wanderings caused amusement to the crane drivers and cupola staff. This may explain why I generally ignored timetabled trains, hence no 'Western' class photographs and precious few Sulzers, these two being, again, on Up trains.

A RARE GLIMPSE AT GREENFORD & NORTHOLT

Plate 159. LNER articulated stock   11th July 1964   Minolta SR1

Plate 160. No.1006 *County of Cornwall*   25th July 1963   Mamiya C22

A rare glimpse indeed of a set of LNER articulated coaches on a Saturday excursion hauled by 'Grange' class loco No.6850. It was a pure chance I had the camera still handy and just caught the two coaches. Despite being July it seems that only the young man wants to take the air.

A mile or so west of Greenford but just shy of Northolt a footbridge crosses over the railway tracks and from this vantage point the following three photographs were taken. Another 4.15pm Bicester working this time a 'County' is in charge, No.1006 *County of Cornwall*.

Plate 161. No.5014 *Goodrich Castle*   9th August 1963   Mamiya C22

Inset: Northolt station c.1961.

Plate 162. No.7021 *Haverfordwest Castle*   7th August 1963   Mamiya C22

Two further 4.15pm Bicester train shots. Photographing the same short train was becoming monotonous but it was the only regular steam working. On both occasions we have 'Castles' in charge, firstly No.5014 *Goodrich Castle* and in the lower picture No.7021 *Haverfordwest Castle*. The cupola stacks and foundry buildings of the British Bath Works make a fine background. The inset picture shows a 'King' class loco on an Up express passing Northolt LT station. The empty ground alongside is now occupied by the Northolt Swimarama, made famous by Terry Wogan on the radio in the 1990s.

The 'King' itself, No.6000 *King George V*, thunders through South Ruislip on an Up train one evening in July 1962. The photograph is Peter Askey's with the old 120 size Kershaw camera. My attempt was an absolute disaster. I had recently started photographing inside Old Oak Common loco shed at around 1/30th sec at full aperture. Reading about an Agfa film rated at 2000ASA I was soon running a film off inside the mirky depths of Old Oak at some ludicrous exposures. The last shot went on our 'King' thundering through South Ruislip.

Whilst Peter was shooting at a respectable f4 @ 1/500sec, I was running at around f16 thinking of a superb low light photograph with excellent depth of field. On developing the film, talk about low light, there was no light, no Old Oak and certainly NO 'King'. Just a transparent film with the slightest hint of sky through an engine shed roof. Apparently I had not heard of something called 'forced' development . . . whatever that was.

Plate 163.   No.6000 *King George V*   July 1962   P.Askey - Kershaw

Plate 164. No.5073 *Blenheim*   30th July 1963   Mamiya C22

Plate 165. No. 5002 *Ludlow Castle*   August 1964   Minolta SR1

West Ruislip station was situated just west of the junction of the former GWR line to Paddington and the former LNER to Marylebone, it was also the terminus of the LT Central Line. The 4.15pm Bicester train features in the top picture with 'Castle' class No.5073 *Blenheim* whilst the lower has a Down special or charter train in the hands of another 'Castle', No.5002 *Ludlow Castle*. The new 1960s build road-level booking hall can be seen with the Down side waiting room cut back to make way for the LT terminus, the footbridge is for London Transport staff only.

Plate 166. No.6995 *Benthall Hall*   Minolta SR1

Plate 167. 'Grange' class loco   Minolta SR1

As with the lower picture on the previous page these two photographs were taken at West Ruislip on a Saturday sometime in August 1964. Peter, Paul, John and myself gathered there on our motorbikes to photograph numerous Down trains running through but what the occasion was I have long forgotten. The top picture has 'Modified Hall' No.6995 *Benthall Hall* with a mixture of GW. LMS and BR Mk I stock whilst a unidentified 'Grange' caught us by surprise on an Up working including a LNER Gresley coach. Even by 1964 the goods yard was still busy,

Plate 168. No.46156   Minolta SR1

Plate 169. No.46156   Minolta SR1

Thanks to 'Mr Net' the 30th July 1964 was a Thursday so I must have been on holiday and spent the afternoon at West Ruislip station. We'll miss the 4.15 for once, anyway my visit was rewarded by 'Royal Scot' No.46156 formerly *The South Wales Borderer* but now nameless on an Up parcels to Marylebone. Hence two photographs. The two cars seen in the station forecourt are a Ford Consul and, I think, an Austin. The goods yard was then a clutter of old buildings including what seems to be a grounded van.

Plate 170. No.D1753   Minolta SR1

Plate 171. No.D1715   Minolta SR1

My intentions at West Ruislip that day were to record main line workings now firmly in the hands of the Sulzer diesel electrics. The top picture, for once neatly composed between a DMU, the footbridge and a signal box but taken to soon, has a Midlands bound express behind No.D1753. The corresponding up, Paddington bound, express has caught No.D1715 with a bit of flair and plenty of station detail. Even the push bike racks are full. The soot marks under the new road level station buildings are clear to see . . . but they will eventually fade.

Plate 172. No.D1727   Minolta SR1

Plate 173. No.D1693   Minolta SR1

Two Up trains both caught at speed. Sulzer diesel electric No.D1727 rattles through with an express goods whilst my attempts to catch the 'Midland Pullman' were to be thwarted. Unknown to me it had been taken out of service for complete overhaul and had been substituted with old Pullman stock. Hence No.D1693. From what I have since read about the riding qualities of the Pullman sets of that period I reckon from the passengers point of view the overhaul could take forever.

Plate 174. No.D255   Minolta SR1

Plate 175. Sulzer Type 2   Minolta SR1

Two surprise workings to me, well surprise in as far that my knowledge of Marylebone train workings were minimal. English Electric Type 4 No.D255 runs through West Ruislip with an Up mixed goods parcels whilst a DMU waits in the station. By 1964 local services out of Marylebone had been in the hands of DMU stock for some time. The Sulzer Type 2 had stopped and must have been on a semi-fast. On the extreme left the London Transport tracks run under the road but that was as far as they went, the original plan to go as far as Denham being abandoned.

Plate 176. No.46112 *Sherwood Forester*   Mamiya C22

Plate 177. No.76038   Mamiya C22

After photographing the 4.15pm Bicester train at West Ruislip, Plate 164, I rode on to Denham to see what remained of the old Uxbridge (High Street) branch where it connected to the main line. I had walked this line some three years previous. Two parcel trains passed whilst there. The first working south, being hauled by 'Royal Scot' class No.46112 *Sherwood Forester* including an LNER Gresley parcels coach which was a great result. BR Standard 2-6-0 No.76038 was working the other way. Whilst photographing it I was so keen for the train to clear the fence I forgot the telegraph pole.

Plate 178. No.48010   P.Wells - Halina 35mm

Plate 179. No.6853   P.Wells - Halina 35mm

Paul Wells and myself travelled on the 4.15pm Bicester train sometime late in 1964, Paul taking photographs along the way. Of my film there is no trace. The LMS '8F' No.48010 is just on the outskirts of Princes Risborough on an Up goods whilst the lower picture shows our train engine 'Grange' class No.6853, sans name and number plates. At least the cab side number has been neatly stencilled on. The semaphore signals make for a interesting photograph. On reflection this was the last time I was hauled by steam locomotive in the sixties.

Plate 180. Oxford Station, looking South   P.Askey - Minolta A5

Plate 181. No.4154   P.Askey - Minolta A5

In years gone by, afore the war, people used to go out at the weekend for what was called a 'spin'. To go for a 'spin' one had to have either a motorbike or a car. You could not 'spin' by walking. Even as late as the sixties us young ones would still go for a 'spin'. So it was that I joined the Askey family one Sunday in June 1963 for a 'spin' in the Hillman Minx to Oxford. In retrospect going out with the Askey family and taking the cameras were the only occasions I went trainspotting by car. Oh, and the two pictures above are taken at the north end of Oxford station.

Plate 182. No.34103 *Calstock*   Mamiya C22

Plate 183. No.4087 *Cardigan Castle*   Mamiya C22

On arrival at Oxford, 'the men' took a walk round the loco shed before finally positioning ourselves up the main line a bit. As to the ladies, Peter's mum and sister, I have not a clue. The two photographs on this page were of a train working up from the south, possibly Bournemouth, and changing locomotives. 'West Country' No.34103 *Calstock* passes under the signal gantry and runs onto the loco depot, whilst 'Castle' class No.4087 *Cardigan Castle* takes the train on northwards and is photographed passing the former closed LMS loco shed.

Plate 184. No.7000 *Viscount Portal*   P.Askey - Minolta A5

Plate 185. No.7031 *Cromwell's Castle*   Mamiya C22

Passenger steam workings through Oxford in the summer of 1963 would be mainly limited to Worcester services. The top picture sees 'Castle' class No.7000 *Viscount Portal* on a Paddington bound express, whilst another 'Castle' No.7031 *Cromwell's Castle* is working a return trip. Both these locomotives have chalked up head codes on their smoke boxes and sadly neither of them would see the year out, in fact No.7031 was withdrawn the following month.

Plate 186. No.5026 *Criccieth Castle*   Mamiya C22

Plate 187. No.6910 *Gossington Hall*   Mamiya C22

Another 'Castle' No.5026 *Criccieth Castle* runs through with a southbound express running parallel to the old LMS line which terminated in Oxford. As can be seen in the lower picture with 'Hall' class No.6910 *Gossington Hall* pulling north out of Oxford station, the old LMS line looks slightly overgrown. At that time, I think it was little used with the old terminus station for goods only and the rails having been removed in the loco shed yard. Curious, but was it not Miss Marple that featured at Gossington Hall when the Bantrys owned the place in Agatha Christie's 'Body in the Library'?

Plate 188. No.6951 *Impney Hall*   Mamiya C22

Plate 189. No.6996 *Blackwell Hall*   Mamiya C22

Judging by the locomotive lamp code, possibly a parcels or empty stock movement in the hands of 'Hall' No.6951 *Impney Hall* moving northwards out of Oxford whilst 'Modified Hall' No.6996 *Blackwell Hall* runs south under the road bridge and onwards into Oxford station. As I recall it was a beautiful summer's day and we spent a pleasant hour or so just photographing trains before facing the wrath of the ladies. Peter Askey's shot of No.7000 shows imagination, whilst Frank's colour transparencies have now degraded to the point where only one survives and features on this book's front cover.

SOUTH WALES MAIN LINE - 12th JULY 1964

Plate 190. No.D6857   Minolta SR1

Plate 191. No.D1055 *Western Advocate*   Minolta SR1

Two photographs 'from the carriage window' taken on 12th July 1964 on a Swansea bound train. English Electric Type 3 No.D6857 hauls an empty wagon train towards Cardiff with Newport steelworks in the distant background. Pulling into Cardiff General station 'Western' class diesel No.D1055 *Western Advocate* waits for the road on a Paddington bound train. Wonder if the little lad in short trousers and notepad in hand wrote many steam train numbers down, by this time they would be few and far between. And he would be in his mid fifties by now.

CARDIFF CANTON DIESEL DEPOT

Plate 192. Cardiff Canton   31st. January 1965   Minolta SR1

Plate 193. Cardiff Canton   12th July 1964   Minolta SR1

Newly completed Cardiff Canton diesel depot photographed from both the Barry and Swansea lines. In the top picture Paul Wells and I are travelling on a local DMU to Barry. The date is 31st. January 1965 and is one of my last train jaunts before calling trainspotting a day. I think the reason is self evident, well one of them anyway. The other view, taken on 12th July 1964, we are Swansea bound but elements of the old order still remain. The semaphore signals have not long to go, and neither have the footbridge and old steam loco shed offices.

Plate 194. Greenford - Ealing Bdy   28th April 1963   F.Askey - Minolta SR3

Plate 195. Paddington - Bicester   October 1964   Minolta SR1

The only two photographs taken of diesel multiple units. The top picture, a two car unit, is near Castle Bar halt on a Greenford to Ealing Broadway service. Peter Askey only took the photograph because he was bored whilst waiting for 'King' class No.6018 on the last 'King' run. The lower picture is of more interest as I was waiting on my girder, courtesy of the British Bath Works, for the 4.15pm out of Paddington. This train was still diagrammed for steam working and the three car DMU surprised me especially as it was beefed up with a GW Hawksworth composite coach.

Plate 196. No.1421   Summer 1961   F.Askey - Kershaw

Plate 197. No.1432   23rd December 1962   Fed-2

My memories of the little '14xx' tanks at work are mainly limited to boarding the train in the bay at Greenford LT station for the Ealing Broadway service. Coaching stock was pure Great Western auto coaches and if I remember correctly they were named. Our top picture shows No.1421 working the 'Marlow Donkey' and was taken by Frank Askey whist out for a Sunday 'spin' with the family. The other of No.1432 was taken by myself at Oswestry station waiting to return to Gobowen after bunking round the shed. The lad looks interested as I am now in the two tone Austin convertible.

Plate 198. No.3721   2nd March 1963   Fed-2

Plate 199. No. 9616   12th July 1964   Minolta SR1

Just two glimpses of something which was an everyday occurrence at one time, pannier tanks going about their mundane duties. My own earliest recollections were of '57xx' panniers shunting the West Ealing goods yard. Pausing on the head shunt under the footbridge known as Jacob's Ladder we could peer down through the open roof hatch to observe the workings below. The top picture has No.3721 shunting coal wagons near to Lydney loco shed and the lower view is of classmate No.9616 around the Newport area

Plate 200. Waterloo departures   Early 1965   P.Wells - Halina 35mm

Plate 201. No.34002 *Salisbury*   P.Askey - Minolta A5

No better place for a start on the Southern Region than Waterloo station, thanks to Paul Wells and Peter Askey. The top picture has Paul pulling away from Waterloo on a suburban train, destination now long forgotten, but the date is sometime in early 1965. He has luckily caught a 'Nelson' EMU, a Bulleid Pacific and a 'Warship' diesel hydraulic. In the far left background is a 'Crompton'.

The enthusiasts give the game away in Peter's picture of 'West Country' class No.34002 *Salisbury*. She heads the first leg of the 'Devonshire Rambler' a Southern Counties Touring Society special.

Plate 202. No.35023   P.Askey - Minolta A5

Plate 203. No.34100 *Appledore*   P.Askey - Minolta A5

We stay with Peter travelling on the SCTS 'Devonshire Rambler'. Mystery still surrounds this steam special as Peter can't remember much about it and 'Mr Net' can tell me anything I want to know about SCTS specials except this one. The date is, I think, sometime 1965/66. If it was a 'last steam down trip Southern main line etc.' it joins a long list of others. 'Merchant Navy' No.35023, now nameless, has arrived at Exeter Central having taken over from our flat top somewhere along the line from Waterloo. 'West Country' class No.34100 *Appledore* is seen at Salisbury on the return leg.

Plate 204. No.34089 *602 Squadron*   Mamiya C22

Plate 205. No.35004 *Cunard White Star*   Mamiya C22

Peter's continual cajoling as to our lack of moving shots precipitated some action so I took myself off one Saturday on the motorbike and stopped off at Clapham and Wandsworth on the way to Nine Elms Loco shed. A Saturday service in the summer months would have been busy and I only spent a few hours by the lineside and rolled off some four films. Then I became bored with it all and went on my way. 'Battle of Britain' class No.34089 *602 Squadron* passes the Peabody Estate, Clapham, on an Up train to Victoria whilst 'Merchant Navy' class No.35004 *Cunard White Star* works a Down West Country express.

CLAPHAM, LONDON - 27th JULY 1963

Plate 206. No.35028 *Clan Line* — Mamiya C22

Plate 207. No.73087 *Linette* — Mamiya C22

Two pictures looking across to St. John's Hill Rise, with an RT bus passing the entrance to Clapham Junction station in the lower picture. Our Victorian terrace housing show the ultimate in respectability, net curtains and an interesting collection at that. At that time window dressing of the more down-at-heel parts of London could boast patterned grease-proof paper to newspapers or even, I recall, old sacking. Giving the washing a good airing is 'Merchant Navy' class No.35028 *Clan Line* on a Bournemouth bound Pullman train, whilst BR Standard Class 5 No.73087 *Linette* is heading for Salisbury.

Plate 208. No.34053 *Sir Keith Park*   Mamiya C22

Plate 209. No.34048 *Crediton*   Mamiya C22

Southern steam versus the power of Daz or OMO washing powders. For the ladies of Strathblane Road, Clapham, Saturday is washing day judging by the whites hanging up to dry in the back gardens alongside the railway. Never let it be said they weren't up to the challenge, the old twin tubs were certainly hard at it that day. 'Battle of Britain' class No.34053 *Sir Keith Park* brings up a Bournemouth train whilst 'West Country' class No.34048 *Crediton* works a Down train to Exeter Central. You have to smile at the optimism of the Strathblaine Road ladies

Plate 210. No.30837   Mamiya C22

Plate 211. No.31617   Mamiya C22

From Clapham we go further down the line to Wandsworth. Judging by the housing we have gone up market despite the fact that on the other side of the cutting was Wandsworth prison. The vast majority of steam locomotives seen that day were in the hands of Southern Pacifics but semi-fast workings produced some interesting variations. Amongst the semi-fast trains that day were 'S15' class No.30837 and 'U' class Mogul No.31617 both working up to Waterloo. Of interest the 'S15' was one of the very last of the class to be withdrawn in September 1965.

Plate 212. No.34017 *Ilfracombe*   Mamiya C22

Plate 213. No.34077 *603 Squadron*   Mamiya C22

Bulleid's rebuilt light Pacifics were easily the most common locomotives seen that day. Of the two examples shown here 'West Country' class No.34017 *Ilfracombe* is working down to Salisbury and Exeter. For the crew of 'Battle of Britain' class No.34077 *601 Squadron* their job is nearly done with Waterloo station only a few miles away. The loco has a full head of steam hence a wisp of steam from the safety valves whilst the tender is partially worked out. The back gardens alongside the railway are more generous and in the rarefied atmosphere of Wandsworth Saturday is not wash day. Perhaps the 'under stairs' staff have the day off.

Plate 214. No.34038 *Lynton*   Mamiya C22

Plate 215. No.34070 *Manston*   Mamiya C22

Unrebuilt examples of Bulleid's light Pacifics were not quite so common and 'West Country' class No.34038 *Lynton* and 'Battle of Britain' class No.34070 *Manston* are both about ten minutes out of Waterloo working West Country express trains. Both locos would have come off Nine Elms loco shed prior to setting off with their tenders full to overflowing. Compare the quantity of coal carried in the tenders of these two locomotives with previous Plate No.213 to roughly work out just how much coal a fireman had to shift. In both cases the trains are made up from period Bulleid stock.

Plate 216. No.35006 *Peninsular & Oriental S.N. Co.*   Mamiya C22

Plate 217. No.35012 *United States Line*   Mamiya C22

The next three pictures feature the rebuilt 'Merchant Navy' class locomotives of which I saw about half the class on that day. All were rebuilt from 1956 and 1959. The top picture has No.35006 *Peninsular & Oriental S.N. Co.* working an Up train of former Southern Railway coaches from Salisbury. In the far background is Wandsworth Prison. This locomotive was the last but one to be rebuilt, and only ran for five years in this form. Meanwhile No.35012 *United States Line* pulls a set of Mk I stock on another West Country service. Clearly viable in this and the following Plate are the Southern Region coaching 'set' numbers.

Plate 218. No.35021 *New Zealand Line*   Mamiya C22

Plate 219. No.73081 *Excalibur*   Mamiya C22

Rebuilt 'Merchant Navy' class No.35021 *New Zealand Line* in a very dirty state although part of the loco cab has been cleaned to reveal the number. The train, comprised of SR Bulleid stock, is 'The Royal Wessex' bound for Bournemouth and Weymouth. British Railways Standard Class 5 No.73081 *Excalibur* is working a stopping train of all Southern stock up from Basingstoke. For the period the cutting seems somewhat overgrown, I would imagine that today it would be a veritable forest.

Plate 220. No.73113 *Lyonnesse*   Mamiya C22

Plate 221. No.73114 *Etarre*   Minolta SR1

Two additional pictures of British Railways Standard Class 5 locomotives, both working the Bournemouth line. The top example is No.73113 *Lyonnesse* pushing out some clag on a Down train, whilst the lower example is No.73114 *Etarre* on an Up train just passing under Heathfield Road bridge. This picture is at variance with the others as it was taken a year later with Paul Wells. We had stopped here for a while before making our way down to take photographs at Redhill. One noticeable thing was the amount of ex-Southern Railway coaching stock still in circulation at that time.

Plate 222. No.31622   Mamiya C22

Plate 223. No.33038   Mamiya C22

Photographing locomotives working light engine do not normally appeal to me, they have always struck me as odd. Something is obviously missing. Southern 'U' class Mogul No.31622 works light through Wandsworth tender first in the Down direction, note the discs on the tender indicating a light engine movement. Meanwhile 'Q1' class No.33038 is passing through Clapham, the rear lamp indicating light engine up to Nine Elms Loco Shed. Note the coal overspill and near empty tender Both these locomotives would be withdrawn six months later.

Plate 224. No.35020 *Bibby Line*   July 1962   F.Askey - Kershaw

Plate 225. 'Schools' class loco   July 1962   F.Askey - Kershaw

Sometime early in June 1962 I accompanied the Askey family to Wimbledon. As Frank, Peter and myself took our cameras we obviously ducked out of the shopping to photograph trains. 'Merchant Navy' class No.35020 *Bibby Line* storms past Wimbledon signal box with a Down southbound Pullman train, note the healthy state of the goods yard. Five minutes later a unidentified 'Schools' class locomotive followed working a semi-fast down to Basingstoke. The chap on the extreme right is me with a Russian made Fed 2. But of my photographs . . . no idea.

Plate 226. No.34028 *Eddystone*   July 1962   F.Askey - Kershaw

Plate 227. No.73016   Early 1965   P.Wells - Halina 35mm

The last of a trio of pictures at Wimbledon, 'West Country' class No.34028 *Eddystone* working up from Basingstoke, note the Southern parcels van tucked in behind the locomotive. The photograph was taken from a narrow footway behind the shops which straddled the railway. Paul Wells' only other photograph taken on his trip from Waterloo in early 1965 was of BR Standard Class 5 No.73016 on a Down local comprised of BR MkI non-corridor stock. This was possibly the only set of this type of stock on the Southern Region. With four tracks in view the shot has to be taken the London side of Basingstoke.

Worting Junction, just west of Basingstoke and where the old Southern Railway line to the South West splits away from the Bournemouth. An imposing shot of 'Merchant Navy' class No.35027 *Port Line* on a Down Bournemouth Pullman train. Pity the locomotive was filthy. As we were all on our motorbikes, after leaving Worting Junction we tracked down some of the long closed stations on the old Basingstoke to Alton line which featured in the Will Hay classic film 'Oh Mr Porter'. Being a beautiful warm summer's day we then wandered off down to Eastleigh loco shed.

Plate 228. No.35027 *Port Line*   Minolta SR1

Plate 229. No.34003 *Plymouth*   Minolta SR1

Plate 230. No.34054 *Lord Beaverbrook*   Minolta SR1

The old Southern Railway main line to the South West ran under the Up Waterloo line from Bournemouth which is on the embankment on the left of the picture. The Down line to Bournemouth is on the extreme right. The two Bulleid Pacifics pictured on this page are both running at speed on South West trains, the first stop being Salisbury. The top picture has rebuilt 'West Country' class No.34003 *Plymouth* with a load of twelve coaches, shortly followed by as built 'Battle of Britain' class No.34054 *Lord Beaverbrook*. Surprisingly, within a month, both locomotives would be withdrawn.

Plate 231. No.34015 *Exmouth*   Minolta SR1

Plate 232. No.34015 *Exmouth*   Minolta SR1

Two photographs taken of the same train, an Up express from the South West heading for Waterloo hauled by 'West Country' class No.34015 *Exmouth*. The Up line to Waterloo from Bournemouth on its embankment is clearly seen on the left of the picture, sadly I seem to have failed to actually photograph the bridge in any great detail. The Southern Railway concrete '143' sign refers to the bridge number, a road which wandered underneath the railway junction.

Plate 233. No.35019 *French Line CGT*   Minolta SR1

Plate 234. No.35022 *Holland America Line*   Minolta SR1

'Merchant Navy' class locomotives Nos.35019 *French Line C.G.T.* and 35022 *Holland America Line* on Bournemouth line expresses. The top picture has No.35019 on the embankment with a Waterloo train whilst No.35022 runs at speed in the opposite direction. I have an excuse for the telegraph pole, we had just arrived and I was still sitting on the bike when she came through. The exact position of the telegraph pole never really came to light until scanning the photograph for this book. By this time I had become attached to the picture, so your disappointment is shared by me.

Plate 235. No.34008 *Padstow*   Minolta SR1

Plate 236. No.31811   Minolta SR1

The picture of 'West Country' class No.34008 *Padstow* on a Bournemouth train posed me with a dilemma. Only I could manage to take a photograph of a moving locomotive with a telegraph pole sticking out of its chimney. One was tempted to ask my publisher to digitally delete it but then he would have to do the other one. Then we would have no telegraph poles at all. Not good. Fellow trainspotter John Durrant seems less than interested as 'N' class No.31811 speeds past on a Up freight. After an hour or so on the old Southern main line things could become somewhat repetitive but even the only Mogul of the day has failed to stir him.

Plate 237. No.7919 *Runter Hall*   Minolta SR1

Plate 238. Nos. 75066 & 30506   Minolta SR1

One could by the 1960s become somewhat bored by the endless flow of Bulleid Pacifics on the Southern. Loco sheds offered greater variety. Then at Worting Junction came these two oddities. 'Modified Hall' class No.7919 *Runter Hall* comes wandering down the Southern main line, safety valve cover missing, the locomotive lamps telling us it's heading for Southampton docks. But what a train, that's what you call a train. Superb positioning re. telegraph pole. Going Salisbury way is BR Standard Class 4 No.75066 hauling a long dead 'S15' No.30506.

EASTLEIGH

Plate 239. No.34077 *603 Squadron*   25th March 1962   Fed-2

Plate 240. No.30902 *Wellington*   25th March 1962   Fed-2

My early efforts around Eastleigh station, all taken on a March 1962 visit to the Works and Loco Shed. 'West Country' class No.34077 *603 Squadron* thunders through the station on an Up express to Waterloo taken after our visit. Was then pulled by a 'Lord Nelson' up to Basingstoke, which I failed to photograph, like a lot of other things. Of the following two photographs, on this page 'Schools' class No.30902 *Wellington* was taken prior to our visit around the Works and I was kicking my heels outside the Works entrance and casually took these shots. Unbelievable.

Plate 241. No.30793 *Sir Ontzlake*   25th March 1962   Fed-2

Plate 242. No.30476   29th October 1961   Kodak 44A

The picture of the 'King Arthur', No.30793 *Ontzlake*, suffers slightly but I think I caught the stringing on the telegraph pole to good effect. Obviously both classes were nearing the end of their days and I'm sure I would have been aware of it. With little or no effort at all much better photographs could easily have been taken. But then I was only sixteen and 400 ASA film didn't help. 'H15' class No.30476 was photographed the previous year with my box camera. My second only shot on the main line since my very first ever attempt. But this time the loco wasn't moving.

Plate 243. Advertising Hoarding   July 1963   P.Askey - Minolta A5

Plate 244. No.30028   August 1962   F.Askey - Kershaw

The following two pages concentrate on the Brockenhurst to Lymington branch, which is still in operation today. Well done Peter in photographing one of the many trackside Strongs Brewery hoardings, this one somewhere in the Brockenhurst area, it would never have entered my head to photograph one. Other hoardings further back would shout 'You are now approaching the Strong Country'. The Askey family were in the Bournemouth area on holiday during August 1962 and Frank caught 'M7' class No.30028 pulling into Brockenhurst station, note the push-pull apparatus fitted to the locomotive.

Plate 245. No.30129   31st. July 1963   P.Askey - Minolta A5

Plate 246. No.30028   August 1962   F.Askey - Kershaw

Two further pictures of 'M7' tanks on the Brockenhurst to Lymington branch. The top picture shows No.30129 pulling away from Brockenhurst during the summer of 1963, whilst the lower has No.30028, again in August 1962, but this time at the other end of the line at Lymington. The old 'M7' tanks were not exactly overloaded with a three coach train of old Maunsell period stock. Within a month of No.30028 being photographed she was withdrawn.

Plate 247. No.34001 *Exeter*   Mamiya C22

Plate 248. No.34098 *Templecombe*   Mamiya C22

With the Askey's holidaying near Bournemouth during the summer of 1963 I motored, or rather motor biked, down to spend a few days with them. On my second day, and with Peter on the pillion, we found an ideal vantage point at Hinton Admiral, just up from the station. On an Up Waterloo train West Country class No.34001 *Exeter* manages a load of twelve Southern coaches and a BR standard parcel van. In the opposite direction, with journey nearly over, another 'West Country' class No.34098 *Templecombe* passes a clear signal.

Plate 249. No.34037 *Clovelly*   Mamiya C22

Plate 250. No.73046   Mamiya C22

Another Up express and again a West Country, this time No.34037 *Clovelly* with an old LNER Gresley coach tucked in behind the tender. Could it have been 'The Pines Express' which had been diverted from the Somerset & Dorset to run via Oxford at the end of the previous summer season? Sadly I have misjudged the moment to press the shutter and only become aware of this some fifty years later. A following Up train, this time a local stopper in the hands of BR Standard Class 5 No.73046. The head shunt and sidings at Hinton Admiral were, at this time, unused.

CHRISTCHURCH - 31st. JULY 1963

Plate 251. No.30836   Mamiya C22

Plate 252. No.31611   Mamiya C22

On my way down to join the Askey family on holiday at the end of July 1963 I stopped off at Christchurch station and spent some time there. At this time semi-fast and local trains could give a greater variety of motive power. These two pictures capture this, both are Bournemouth trains, the top picture showing 'S15' class No.30836 just pulling off whilst the lower picture has 'U' class No.31611 coming under the B3073, passing the signal box and approaching the station. 'Car Mart', the car and accessory shop on the corner has, for the time, a rather American feel to it.

Plate 253. No.34034 *Honiton*

Mamiya C22

Plate 254. No.34061 *73 Squadron*

Mamiya C22

The Up 'Bournemouth Belle' Pullman has just passed through the station and approaches the road bridge. The day was hot and sunny and the signalman has his window open and can be seen at work. What a way to travel by train, just lay back and soak up Pullman style luxury and dream on with a steam engine up front beating the way. On this occasion 'West Country' No.34034 *Honiton* does the work and the crew no doubt dreaming of some generous tips. On another Up train we have a close up view of 'Battle of Britain' class No.34061 *73 Squadron*, a high shutter speed here concealing a wee bit of wheel spin.

Plate 255. No.34004 *Yeovil*   Mamiya C22

Plate 256. No.34082 *615 Squadron*   Mamiya C22

Platform level at Christchurch station. 'West Country' class No.34004 *Yeovil* waits for the off whilst on a later Down train 'Battle of Britain' class No.34082 *615 Squadron* prepares to pull off. Bulleid Pacifics were somewhat 'light on their feet' and too much 'welley' when starting off could result in dramatic wheel spinning, but not a lot else. I once owned a motorbike like that, a single cylinder BSA 499cc Gold Star Clubman. Starting off was similar to a 'spam cam', clutch in, plenty of throttle furiously slipping clutch and much noise . . . but not a lot else.

Plate 257. No.35005 *Canadian Pacific*   Mamiya C22

Plate 258. No.35012 *United States Line*   Mamiya C22

Two pictures of 'Merchant Navies' taken at either end of Christchurch station. Top picture shows a grubby No.35005 *Canadian Pacific* leaving a trail of soot heading towards Bournemouth, whilst No.35012 *United States Line*, safety valves lifting, ducks under the main A35 road. The track for the Up bay platform has been lifted. Whilst sitting on the grass a man bolted straight across the tracks hotly pursued by a young bobby waving his truncheon. I took a picture. Can't show it because I posted the negative to the local 'nick'. Never heard anything, but I bet it gave them a laugh.

Plate 259. No.75067   Mamiya C22

Plate 260. No.92001   Mamiya C22

An Up local train in the hands of BR Standard Class 4 No.75067 giving a nicely balanced shot with a telegraph pole. You think not, OK then. Photographed just to the east of Christchurch station BR Standard Class 9F No.92001 heads Bournemouth way with a cement train. Strangely enough I was most surprised to see a 9F down this way. I don't know why, it's just that I was. Having spent an enjoyable hour or so in the of company of smoke and smuts I jumped on the old bike down to Mudeford but an oily blue haze came with me. Along with the smoke and smuts, not uncommon for the time.

Plate 261. No.31623   Mamiya C22

Plate 262. No.35021 *New Zealand Line*   Mamiya C22

On my last day on holiday I deserted the bike and travelled by train from Christchurch into Bournemouth stopping for a short while at Pokesdown. 'U' class No.31623 dropped me off on a somewhat deserted station just in time to catch the Up 'Bournemouth Belle' which went through in grand style something which always accompanied the passing of a Pullman train. In the late 1950s and early 1960s all things railway could still be dirty and drab but by God a Pacific steam locomotive pulling a set of Pullman cars could lift the spirits. Even if you could never afford such travel.

Plate 263. No.34053 *Sir Keith Park*   Mamiya C22

Plate 264. No.34053 *Sir Keith Park*   Mamiya C22

A Down Bournemouth train stops at Pokesdown this time with 'Battle of Britain' class No.34053 *Sir Keith Park* in charge. The photograph was taken moments after the train's arrival and the station porter seems to be casually eyeing the platform up and down for a potential tip from hard pressed holidaymakers. No such luck. The only other punter present on the platform would appear to be waiting for someone. The following picture features the same train with the loco crew awaiting the guard's flag so they can be on their way.

Plate 265. No.34028 *Eddystone*   Mamiya C22

Plate 266. No.34104 *Bere Alston*   P.Askey - Minolta A5

'West Country' class No.34028 *Eddystone* heads an Up train photographed, I think, from the road bridge in the far distance in the preceding plate. Note the virtual lack of vehicles on the road to the left of the picture. Having travelled in to Bournemouth Central station I quickly bunked round the loco shed and then, time pressing, headed back to Christchurch and then onto my bike for home, holiday over. Peter had bunked the shed and spent some time at the station a few days earlier, catching 'West Country' class No.34104 *Bere Alston* just pulling out as he arrived.

BOURNEMOUTH - 25th JULY 1963

Plate 267. No.34014 *Budleigh Salterton*   P.Askey - Minolta A5

Plate 268. No.34029 *Lundy*   P.Askey - Minolta A5

As far as this book goes it was just as well a young Peter evaded his parents whilst on holiday and headed for Bournemouth Central station, what better way to spend your time than trainspotting and photographing trains. Four pictures of Bulleid's light Pacifics around the station. On this page 'West Country' class No.34014 *Budleigh Salterton* backs in with empty coaching stock from Bournemouth West whilst another 'West Country' No.34029 *Lundy* works in from the West station with a Waterloo express. The corrugated 'shack' on the right is an extension to the locomotive depot.

Plate 269. No.34077 *603 Squadron*   P.Askey - Minolta A5

Plate 270. No.34090 *Sir Eustace Missenden*   P.Askey - Minolta A5

'Battle of Britain' class locomotives feature on this page. Firstly and yet again, No.34077 *603 Squadron* has arrived at Bournemouth Central and will be working on down to Weymouth. In the right background can be seen the high-level signal box located on the Down arrivals platform. Classmate No.34090 *Sir Eustace Missenden* has worked a Down train to Bournemouth West and is returning light engine and running past the original loco shed. Sadly whilst Peter spent several hours at Bournemouth Central no 'flat top' deemed to put in an appearance.

Plate 271. No.35011 *General Steam Navigation*   P.Askey - Minolta A5

Plate 272. No.35030 *Elder Dempster Line*   P.Askey - Minolta A5

The pride of the Southern, Bulleid's 'Merchant Navy' class. The top picture features No.35011 *General Steam Navigation* on an Up train off Bournemouth West and now running past the locomotive shed prior to stopping at Bournemouth Central. No.35030 *Elder-Dempster Lines* would seem to be running into Bournemouth Central station but her tender seems suspiciously low on coal so she may be bringing in empty stock.

BOURNEMOUTH - 25th JULY 1963

Plate 273. No.73086

P.Askey - Minolta A5

Plate 274. Nos.76027 & 76062

P.Askey - Minolta A5

British Railways' Standard classes were much in evidence during our stay around Bournemouth and Peter has caught Class 5 No.73086 *The Green Knight* working in from Bournemouth West with an Up semi-fast to Waterloo. On the down 'through' road Class 4 No.76027 waits its next turn of duty whilst classmate No.76062 will shortly be heading for Weymouth. Bournemouth Central station was some way from the sea and during the summer months the taxi trade would have done a roaring trade. For the less affluent there was the bus but for many it would have been 'shanks pony'.

Plate 275. No.31808

P.Askey - Minolta A5

Plate 276. No.80065

P.Askey - Minolta A5

Despite the never ending flow of passenger traffic through Bournemouth Central, freight workings did occur and in the top picture class 'N' No.31808 works a Down freight through towards Poole. The lower picture depicts BR Standard Class 4 tank No.80065 working a short Up cement train past the loco shed. Note the difference in building styles between, on the right, the original and the latter day rear extension.

BOURNEMOUTH - 25th JULY 1963

Plate 277. No.30127   P.Askey - Minolta A5

Plate 278. Nos.30036 & 75078   P.Askey - Minolta A5

The Drummond 'M7' tanks were common around the Bournemouth area as late as 1963 being employed either on local branch line workings or general duties. By 1964 they would be gone. The top picture has No.30127 working a single van alongside a BR Standard 9F in the loco yard whilst fellow classmate No.30036 coupled with BR Standard 4 No.75078 comes up light engine from Bournemouth West running onto the loco shed. Both these 'M7s' pictured here have only months of service left, No.30127 hung on to year's end and No.30036 just made it into 1964.

Plate 279. No.34006 *Bude*   P.Askey - Kershaw

Plate 280. No.30057   P.Askey - Kershaw

A few more Askey holiday shots, Bournemouth again, but the year before, 1962. Frank had the new 35mm
SLR so Peter was let loose with the old 120 Kershaw. The top picture has unrebuilt 'West Country' class
No.34006 *Bude* drifting into Central station on an Up Waterloo bound train passing a Crompton diesel in
the loco yard. Push-pull working 'M7' class No.30057 sits on the Down through road waiting her next turn,
she has a red lamp on the left hand buffer beam so is possibly working Bournemouth West and Wimborne
way.

TEN MINUTES AT BRANKSOME - 17th MAY 1964

Plate 281. No.34038 *Lynton*   P.Askey - Minolta A5

Plate 282. No.34038 *Lynton*   P.Askey - Minolta A5

An overnight motorbike trip to Bournemouth and Weymouth in May1964. We left home around midnight, stopped off in the early hours at a café on the A30 and had breakfast in Bournemouth. Popped round to the West station, which was empty, and then on to Branksome. Whilst poking about, 'West Country' class No.34038 *Lynton* worked past on a Waterloo bound train, the top picture showing the junction with the Dorset line. The sole occupants of the loco depot were a line of dead 'M7' tanks, note the old shovel thrown down in the lower picture. If only a shovel could tell a tale . . .

Plate 283. No.W17 *Seaview*   P.Askey - Minolta A5

Plate 284. No.W17 *Seaview*   P.Askey - Minolta A5

Peter Askey and Paul Wells spent a few days on the Isle of Wight in August 1963, sadly I had to work so that was that. Tales of spending the night on a park bench didn't impress me at the time. The little 'O2' tanks were transferred over to the Island from the 1920s onwards, the last being transferred in 1949. Whilst their classmates on the mainland had all been withdrawn by 1963 these examples worked on till 1967. The carriage stock was a mixture of SE&CRly and LB&SCRly. The two pictures above show No.W17 *Seaview* at Sandown station on a Ventnor to Ryde train.

Plate 285. No.W28 *Ashey*
P.Askey - Minolta A5

Plate 286. No.W28 *Ashey*
P.Askey - Minolta A5

Two more pictures on the Ventnor to Ryde line. No.*W28 Ashey* heads towards Shanklin on a Ryde train passing the Lower Hyde caravan site. Seems that one of the caravans has lost its wheels, perhaps rendering it a permanent fixture. Caravan sites in the 1960s could host the most motley collections of old tat that would make a scrap yard look respectable. In the lower picture Shanklin town forms a backdrop as No.*W28 Ashey* rolls in on a Ventnor train. The 'O2' tanks working the Island differed from their mainline classmates in having heightened bunkers.

Plate 287. No.W24 *Calbourne*   P.Askey - Minolta A5

Plate 288. No.W14 *Fishbourne*   P.Askey - Minolta A5

Still on the Ventnor to Ryde line, this time at Ryde St. Johns station with class 'O2' No.W24 *Calbourne* working in from Ryde Pier with a Ventnor train. In the lower picture No.W14 *Fishbourne* waits prior to setting off with another Ventnor train. The railway works are situated alongside the station and can just be seen on the right of this picture. Whilst travelling up from Basingstoke to Reading sometime in 1964 I witnessed, set down from the main line, sidings full of old rusty London Transport Central Line stock. Scrap, or potential IOW stock. Any takers?

Plate 289. No.W35 *Freshwater*   P.Askey - Minolta A5

Plate 290. No.W35 *Freshwater*   P.Askey - Minolta A5

Having wandered around the loco shed at Ryde the next destination was a ride over to Cowes. No.W35 *Freshwater* simmers quietly at the end of Ryde St. Johns station just before pulling out. A lunch break was called for at Cowes and *Freshwater* is again caught coming into the station on a later working. Strangely enough this was the only member of the class I ever saw whilst on a family day excursion to the Isle of Wight sometime in the mid 1950s. On arrival by ferry at Ryde we strolled down the pier my little bonus being witnessing *Freshwater's* arrival with her train of red coaches.

Plate 291. No.34064 *Fighter Command*   31st. July 1963   Mamiya C22

Plate 292. No.828 *Magnificent*   August 1969   Iris's Box Thing

Going Bournemouth way for a few days holiday during the summer of 1963 I went via Salisbury the plan being to 'do' the shed. Sadly I got thrown out. Whilst hanging around the station I caught 'Battle of Britain' class No.34064 *Fighter Command* on an Exeter bound train. On the outer reaches of this book, 1969, I travelled down with Iris my fiancée from Waterloo to the West Country for a holiday. The old Southern main line was already but a shadow of its former self, and Iris poses in front of a blue 'Warship' class No.828 *Magnificent* at a somewhat downgraded Yeovil Junction station.

Plate 293. 'Warship' class loco   Halina 35mm

Plate 294. 'Warship' class loco   Halina 35mm

Continuing from the previous page, two pictures admittedly 'out of time' for this book. Taken in June 1970, two unidentified 'Warship' class diesel hydraulics on the downgraded Exeter service from Waterloo. Caught a few miles east of Crewkerne, the top picture is from Kingswood Farm bridge and shows the singling of the old main line. The stretch of track here was the first length of all welded rail laid, known locally as the 'Golden Mile'. The lower view was taken slightly to the east of the above, any hopes of photographing here today would be dashed, trees and bushes all but hiding the line.

Plate 295. No.D855 *Triumph*   6th September 1964   Minolta SR1

Plate 296. No.D814 *Dragon*   6th September 1964   Minolta SR1

Four photographs taken at Exeter (St. Davids) station. By September 1964 the 'Warship' diesel hydraulics had just started to replace steam on the Southern main line to Waterloo. Time was at a premium as my train from Paddington didn't get me down to Exeter till the early afternoon. Having to work out what bus to take me on to Exmouth Junction loco shed I did catch two 'Warships' around the station, No.D855 *Triumph* was idling in the now closed, GW loco shed yard whilst classmate No.D814 *Dragon* runs on to its train prior to setting off for Waterloo. Then I was off to Taunton.

Plate 297. No.34084 *253 Squadron*   27th February 1964   Mamiya C22

Plate 298. No.41295   6th September 1964   Minolta SR1

On the day this photograph was taken, February 1964, steam still ruled the roost on the old Southern main line between Exeter and Waterloo. Unrebuilt 'Battle of Britain' class No.34084 *253 Squadron* pulls smartly out of St. Davids station the steam sadly obscuring the famous semaphore signal gantry. The lower picture shows the said gantry to some effect, Ivatt tank No.41295 runs through the station with a mixed goods obscuring a 'Western' diesel hydraulic. The picture is something of a bonus as it was heavily over exposed. Such are the wonders of the digital age,

Plate 299. No.31634   Mamiya C22

Plate 300. No.31633   Mamiya C22

Two photographs taken in quick succession in the loco yards of Reading motive power depot. 'U' class Mogul No.31634 works a train of empty mineral wagons round Reading's southern curve towards Basingstoke. Minutes later fellow class mate No.31633 ran light engine around the curve and through the station onto the Southern loco shed. What was of interest in the top picture was a ganger standing close by the track, he really made the picture. As the camera was held on a tilt straightening up the picture on the scanner resulted in our ganger being lost. Now in the old days . . .

Plate 301. No.7808 *Cookham Manor*   Minolta SR1

Plate 302. No.30543   Minolta SR1

Paul rode pillion to me down to Redhill in the summer of 1964 as his 250cc Honda had again expired due to over exuberance. For once, I seem to recall, we were aware of steam's demise on the Redhill to Reading line. The two pictures both bring the 1960s into sharp focus with new building work going on that will change Redhill's skyline forever. 'Manor' class No.7808 *Cookham Manor* sets off for Reading carrying a spare safety valve cover on the tender whilst 'Q' class No.30543 was shunting a train of ballast wagons.

Plate 303. No.31816   Minolta SR1

Plate 304. No.31816   Minolta SR1

Neatly framed between the signalbox and a Crompton diesel, 'N' class Mogul No.31816 runs into Redhill with a Reading train. The signalbox is set in the fork of the Brighton and Guildford lines. Having uncoupled from her train No.31816 runs back light engine through the station although in this picture she would appear totally crewless. Redhill at the time was much smaller town and on the ride down I remember descending Box Hill on the old Brighton road. Steep. Afore the war my dad had the brakes fail on a lorry there and only managed to grind to a halt by continuously ramming the kerb.

Plate 305. No.31791   Minolta SR1

Plate 306. No.76034   Minolta SR1

'U' class Mogul No.31791 runs through Redhill station on a ballast train with a ballast plough set behind the
locomotive, the Crompton still sits comfortably idling away waiting for its next duty. BR Standard Class 4
No.76034 approaches Redhill station with another Reading service, I remember thinking that the variety of
steam on offer here far eclipsed the Waterloo main line. This particular train also offers some variety with,
immediately behind the locomotive, two vans firstly one of LMS origin followed by an LNER six wheeler,
the train itself comprising of BR MkI stock.

Plate 307. No.80094   Minolta SR1

Plate 308. No.80094   Minolta SR1

Four pictures of BR Standard Class 4 tanks featuring Nos.80094 and 80095. To a setting of cranes and the 'new order' it has to be said that No. 80094 does not sit too well. Far better the Crompton diesel to set that scene. Whatever, she has just come off shed and the lower view has her on a Tonbridge train comprised of 1920s Maunsell 'Continental' stock. In putting this book together many years after the event it is a great pity I took no interest in the great variety of coaching stock then on offer. Oddly enough I do remember roof periscopes fitted to some old stock. Why?

Plate 309. No.80095   Minolta SR1

Plate 310. No.80095   Minolta SR1

BR Standard tank No.80095 arrives with a Reading service, this time with a train of early 1930s Maunsell narrow bodied Hastings stock. Having worked into the station she has run round her train and waits momentarily before running on to the loco depot. Our young fireman takes a breather, he definitely looks of 'Rocker' ilk, perhaps the proud owner of a big BSA or Triumph motorbike in the yard. Of the locomotives caught on our little sojourn at Redhill all managed to survive for a few more years except, surprisingly, No.76034 which was withdrawn two months later.

By the summer of 1963 'Coronation' class locomotives were not so common on the Euston main line being employed on various secondary duties, relief workings, parcel and covering diesel failures. A lucky shot of No.46225 *Duchess of Gloucester* heading north taken from Camden loco shed. Only two other 'Coronations' were on that day surrounded by hoards of English Electric Type 4s. Steam was on its last legs. As per the 1960s cranes and scaffolding are out and about, but the roof of Camden's old roundhouse can be seen as indeed it can be today.

Plate 311. No.46225 *Duchess of Gloucester*   7th July 1963   Mamiya C22

Plate 312. No.46517   28th April 1963   Minolta SR1

Plate 313. AC electric loco   1966   Minolta SR1

Both pictures feature the Euston main line at Willesden, the top taken from the junction of Station and Harley Road in 1963. The cooling towers dominate the loco shed roundhouse and coaling plant which all makes for a dramatic background to the Ivatt Mogul. Note Cinema Coach No.2 in the sidings. The lower picture was taken just three years later at the top end of the old carriage sidings alongside Harley Road, shortly after the introduction of the overhead electrification. Willesden's old steam shed stood silent and empty. Not a soul stirred.

Plate 314. No.48632   Mamiya C22

Plate 315. No.48656   Mamiya C22

When quite young my mother occasionally took me to Wembley. I was allowed to explore and always retained this vague childlike memory of a long footbridge spanning the railway tracks. Whilst around Wembley many years later I went looking for my 'mystery' footbridge, it was south of Wembley Central station off of Lyon Park Road. A couple of '8F's were chuntering about. Many years later my eldest daughter Georgina found my father's lost family on the Internet and through the '50s and '60s they lived at Lyon Park Road. A story that has not a lot to with railways though.

Plate 316. No.70033 *Charles Dickens*   25th May 1963   P.Askey - Minolta A5

Plate 317. No.70017 *Arrow*   25th May 1963   Mamiya C22

Opposite the road entrance to Wembley Central station and between the shops was a set of dirty narrow steep steps which led down to a 'bombsite' car park alongside the Euston main line, ideal for spotting. By 1963 it was being built on so Peter discovered another good spot just up the line where the Great Central line crossed over and where I joined him on Cup Final day, Saturday 25th May. Several 'Britannias' put in appearances with two pictured here No.70033 *Charles Dickens* on the Slow lines with a northbound train while No.70017 *Arrow* works into Euston with a Up Fast.

Plate 318. No.46229 *Duchess of Hamilton*   May 1963   P.Askey - Minolta A5

Plate 319. No.46239 *City of Chester*   11th May 1963   P.Askey - Minolta A5

Previous to the Cup Final Saturday Peter had ventured up to Wembley on the 11th May for the Rugby League Cup and was rewarded with three passing 'Coronation' Pacifics. For 1963 this was impressive and two of those 'Coronation' shots are featured here. No.46229 *Duchess of Hamilton* presents a steamy shot as she runs under the Great Central main line on a northbound express whilst sister 'Coronation' No.46239 *City of Chester* hoves into view on an Up express possibly from the Midlands. Despite Peter's optimism the following Cup Final day produced no 'Coronations' whatsoever.

Plate 320. No.46335 *City of Birmingham*   11th May 1963   P.Askey - Minolta A5

Plate 321. No.46335 *City of Birmingham*   11th May 1963   P.Askey - Minolta A5

Of the three 'Coronations' seen on Rugby League Cup day, 11th May 1963, No.46235 *City of Birmingham* was working a charter train being caught twice in both directions. The top picture is a morning shot as *City of Birmingham* runs into Euston on the Slow lines with the Up charter train, whilst later that day she was caught on the return working. The building site, right background, was where we would once sit by our pushbikes trainspotting, with on one occasion, a '2P' engineman throwing his tea slops all over us.

Plate 322. No.46115 *Scots Guardsman*   11th May 1963   P.Askey - Minolta A5

Plate 323. No.46140 *The Kings Royal Rifle Corps* 25th May 1963 P.Askey - Minolta A5

Whilst 'Coronation' class Pacifics were in decline 'Royal Scots', 'Jubilees' and 'Patriots' were much in evidence. Two pictures of 'Royal Scots' feature here, No.46115 *Scots Guardsman* working an Up charter train and No.46140 *The Kings Royal Rifle Corps* on a Midland region express. Both trains are running on the Slow lines with paper on board headcodes being the order of the day. The telegraph poles sit well with the trains but the 'U' shape concrete tunnel sections thrown down by the trackside when finally set in position will bring an end to those archaic wooden poles.

Plate 324. No.45523 *Bangor*   11th May 1963   P.Askey - Minolta A5

Plate 325. No.45530 *Sir Frank Ree*   11th May 1963   P.Askey - Minolta A5

Another northbound or Down charter train on the Slow running lines, this time in the capable hands of rebuilt 'Patriot' No.45523 *Bangor*. Leaving Wembley Central station behind the shop backs in Wembley High Road which crosses over the main running lines form a fitting backdrop. From a different view another rebuilt 'Patriot', this time an immaculate No.45530 *Sir Frank Ree* on a northbound train makes a splendid sight as she goes under the Great Central's main running lines. *Sir Frank Ree* has had the attention of the Willesden cleaners. And as for how Peter actually got to this perch . . . don't ask.

Plate 326. No.45672 *Anson*   25th May 1963   Mamiya C22

Plate 327. No.45705 *Seahorse*   11th May 1963   P.Askey - Minolta A5

The girder bridge of the Great Central running lines forms a dramatic setting for these two pictures of 'Jubilee' class locomotives, Nos.45672 *Anson* and 45705 *Seahorse*. *Anson* is working a Euston express on the main Up running lines and unlike Down trains the steam locomotives do not appear to be working hard. The lower picture shows *Seahorse* at work going northwards on the Slow lines, showering smoke and steam as she goes underneath the girder bridge. Note the bridge smoke deflectors under the main running lines as well as on the signal gantry.

Plate 328. No.44766   25th May 1963   Mamiya C22

Plate 329. No.44831   11th May 1963   P.Askey - Minolta A5

Noting the locomotive train headcodes displayed at Wembley most indicate various destinations or charter trains. However a clean 'Black 5' class No.44766 runs on the Up main on Cup Final day under headcode '1X72' which may make it a Cup Final Special. Not only that but of all the trains photographed that day this particular one is made up of clean MkI stock, so it can't be a football special. Can it? Another Up working taken two weeks earlier has 'Black 5' No.44831 working into Euston. Our old driver, who prefers his own cap, is perhaps keeping a watchful eye on his fireman in the drivers seat.

Plate 330. No.45414   25th May 1963   Mamiya C22

Plate 331. No.45434   11th May 1963   P.Askey - Minolta A5

Two more shots of 'Black 5s', the top picture with No.45414 working an Up mixed goods on the Slow lines whilst the lower one has No.45434 on a Down northbound express on the Main. For those with a sporting interest the 1963 Cup Final was between Manchester City and Leicester. Due to the hard winter in 1963 this match had been postponed several times finally being played on the 25th May. Oh, and Manchester won. The Rugby League match, two weeks previous, was between Wigan Warriors and Wakefield, the Warriors lost.

Plate 332. No.48284   25th May 1963   P.Askey - Minolta A5

Plate 333. No.48284   25th May 1963   P.Askey - Minolta A5

The other great mainstay of the old LMS was Stanier's '8F'. Although photographed on Cup Final day these two views of '8F' No.48284 was pulling no football special but a trainload of empty mineral wagons heading north. Framed by the Great Central overbridge the proximity of the houses so close to the running tracks is apparent. Just imagine the joys of living in Acacia Avenue, Wembley. Not only having the sound and smell of the railway you would feel its presence. Times of trains would be known as cups and saucers gently shook, light vibrations causing ripples in one's tea.

Plate 334. No.48506   25th May 1963   Mamiya C22

Plate 335. No.78034   May 1963   P.Askey - Minolta A5

Another '8F' slogs on through with a Down goods, the locomotive lampcode indicates an 'express freight' but it hardly looks that way. The second wagon back is a container flat with its container. Goods yards large and small could easily deal with these, they were crane handled with shackles on the roof and were common on mixed goods or formed complete trains. Meanwhile two long concrete beams form a heavy load for a couple of bogie bolsters pulled by BR Standard Class 2 No.78034 on the Down Main.

Plate 336. No.DP2   11th May 1963   P.Askey - Minolta A5

Plate 337. English Electric Type 4   25th May 1963   P.Askey - Minolta A5

Our two visits to the lineside at Wembley in May 1963, produced many diesel hauled trains, sadly mostly ignored. Peter photographed two, which are both published and I failed to take any. Only one 120 film. The top picture is a classic one of DP2 working an Up express into Euston. Introduced in May 1962 this was a lucky shot as she was transferred to the Eastern Region a few months later. The lower picture has an unidentified English Electric Type 4 working an Up parcels train. She must be an early build with split head codes and front access with small yellow warning panel.

Plate 338. No.45622 *Nyasaland*   25th May 1963   Mamiya C22

Plate 339. No.45739 *Ulster*   11th May 1963   P.Askey - Minolta A5

With two big sporting events at Wembley, the Rugby League and Football Finals many specials and charter trains worked 'over the top' on the old Great Central line to Marylebone. Working an Up Cup Final special on the 25th May is 'Jubilee' class No.45622 *Nyasaland* whereas on a return working after the Rugby League cup on the 11th May is another 'Jubilee' No.45739 *Ulster*. She was one of the last to be withdrawn in 1967. Note the trainspotters 'trespassing' on the bridge parapet. We never bothered anyone, and nobody bothered us. Little rascals . . .

Plate 340. No.45598 *Basutoland*   25th May 1963   P.Askey - Minolta A5

Plate 341. No.45658 *Keyes*   11th May 1963   P.Askey - Minolta A5

Two more 'Specials' on the old Great Central and like its Euston counterpart a smoke box mounted paper head board 'X' indicates a special working. With the girder bridge behind us we have 'Jubilee' No.45598 *Basutoland* on train 1X64 apparently a Leicester to Wembley Hill Cup Final special. As a fitting end to two great sporting events I noticed in this picture that as our' Jubilee' is about to rumble over the Euston main line one of the engine crew is pointing out towards the stadium, except on consulting the London 'A to Z' the stadium would appear to be on the other side.

Plate 342. No.D292   Minolta SR1

Plate 343. No.D377   Minolta SR1

Just over a year later we reprised our perch alongside the Euston main line at Wembley to take a few photographs to record any changes that had occurred. The electric overhead gantry is in, although not yet active, and all the cabling is set to ground level in concrete trunking. English Electric Type 4 diesels now dominate on the Euston main line with No.D292 heading a Down northbound express comprised of LMS stock whilst No.D377 is on an Up Euston pulling BR MkIs. This stranglehold of EE Type 4 diesels was short-lived, the overhead becoming 'live' two years later.

Plate 344. No.D5074   Minolta SR1

Plate 345. No.73013   Minolta SR1

With both the driver and guard keeping a careful look out, Sulzer No.D5074 with disc indicators and small yellow warning panel reverses a six-wheel LMS parcel van and wagons into the yards behind Wembley Central station. Our time at Wembley was limited but I recall only two steam locomotives, an '8F' pulling a brake van and the BR Class 5 No.73013 running light. The end house has the bedroom window open something the occupants might be more able to do, the back garden being simple but tidy. Perhaps the shed was a pigeon 'loft'.

Plate 346. No.73038   Minolta SR1

Inset: The Iron Bridge, North Circular Road, Neasden, c.1960s.

(Courtesy After the Battle, Photographer Arthur Ingram)

Plate 347. No.46165   Minolta SR1

Following our short stay at stay at Wembley we nipped round to Neasden and found, down on the old Great Central main line doing a bit of shunting, BR Standard Class 5 No. 73038. Stooging about unsure if anything would appear a now nameless 'Royal Scot' No.46165 swung of the GC line and onto the spur joining up with the Midland to West London line. In the background the North Circular Road and its infamous iron bridge can be seen, off right of the picture was a succession of slow and fast bends on which several 'ton up' lads, including nearly me, came to grief.

Plate 348. No.46165

Minolta SR1

Another view of our 'Royal Scot' No.46165 formerly named *The Ranger*. Within four months she would be withdrawn and barely make 1965 before being cut up. The scrap yard has an interesting collection of cars which may possibly outlive our 'Royal Scot'. The building behind is not Neasden loco shed which was on the opposite side of the railway tracks, and by now long closed. Neasden to me, when young, meant going by bus up the North Circular Road to visit my mum's family. Once aboard the number 112 it was top deck all the way and I would settle in the front seat as we would soon dive under the five railway arches at Stonebridge Park. Excitement would mount as we then approached Neasden's great girder railway over bridge, known locally as 'the iron bridge'. With railway sidings and goods depots approaching on the left, the railwaymen's allotments and loco shed with two coaling plants would soon come into view on the other side of the road with a great smoky pall hanging in the air. Occasionally a Metropolitan electric locomotive and train rattled past. To a young Teddy this place was magic.

KING'S CROSS - FAST FORWARD TO 1977

After my last visit to King's Cross with the Askeys in 1962 I returned in March 1977 and took the above photograph. The famous signal box which went out of use in the early 1970s had already gone, the last vestiges of the old signalling remain and York Road platform had finally closed that month. But now back to our memories . . .

RETURN TO KING'S CROSS - SEPTEMBER 1961

Plate 349. No.60026 *Miles Beevor*   P. Wells - Kodak 44A

If you're a Harry Potter person then these few pages are my platform nine and a half moment. If I though for one moment that if I charged at one of King's Cross brick arches I'd land up in the land of these pictures I'd have a go. But to see a Great Western 'Hall' painted red at King's Cross . . . , er, no thanks, give that one a miss then.

These few pictures were are taken by Paul Wells, aged fourteen, in September 1961 on his Kodak 44A box camera. They are magic to me because I wasn't there to take them. It's as simple as that. None of my own photographs have any real magic, plenty of interest, but no magic. Those that are lost are mourned after. The great days of steam are always the ones witnessed before owning a camera. Taking ones own photographs seems to destroy the magic of being at these places, perhaps that just means I'm not creative as a photographer. Paul's powerful close up photograph of 'A4' class No.60026 *Miles Beevor* fits in with a box camera's square negative format, even to the point of chopping off the tender. Wasn't me governor!.

Plate 350. No.60014 *Silver Link*   P.Wells - Kodak 44A

Plate 351. No.60028 *Walter K Whigham*   P.Wells - Kodak 44A

Two further A4s photographed by Paul that day in September 1961. The top picture shows No.60014 *Silver Link* whilst the lower, which is more akin for a box camera, has No.60028 *Walter K. Whigham*. Even then these two A4s are just over a year away from the chop. The year Paul took these photos would find me waiting by an archway on the corner of York Road, King's Cross for the Home Counties Railway Club's coach. Trips sometimes kicked off from there and on one occasion I witnessed three A4s set back from each other at the buffer stops. I remember fingering the old 44A box camera . . . no, better to snap a another pannier tank on another shed.

Plate 352. No.60148 *Aboyeur*   P.Wells - Kodak 44A

Plate 353. No.60065 *Knight of the Thistle*   P.Wells - Kodak 44A

'A1' class locomotive No.60158 *Aberdonian* runs into King's Cross, to an imposing but simple, 1930s backdrop including a just discernable mineral wagon which, if memory proves correct, was for station rubbish. Meanwhile with the superb setting of King's Cross signalbox 'A3' class No.60065 *Knight of the Thistle* arrives with an Up express, already boasting a double chimney but as yet, to have the German style smoke deflectors fitted. And talking of German smoke deflectors brings us to about where we came in.

DEJA-VU

As already mentioned railway photography restarted in the 1970s as some form of physical therapy following an industrial accident. Trainspotting through the late 1950s onwards I had failed to grasp that the identities of the British Railways regions held more to their pre-Nationalisation companies than I realised. Time had moved on and by the mid 1970s what become apparent was that the old regions had given way to a uniform, even bland, British Rail which was then going through its blue period. Diesel locos were familiar to me even if the numbers were not, some classes worked on the wrong regions and surprisingly some had already disappeared. However although 'spotting' had passed its sell by date I was soon at home snapping away even if I then became quickly aware of having to add a broken left wrist to my other problems. Married to Iris in 1970 we holidayed many times in Cornwall which led to a great interest in, and photographing, Cornish Tin Mines which led once again to a 35mm camera. This was to be history repeating itself with yet another Kodak Retinette 1A followed by a new SLR, but this time an Asahi Pentax KX. By this time colour film was well established and the camera was used for railway photography as well as the families happy snaps. A 120 format twin lens reflex was eventually purchased with black & white photography in mind but the darkroom side never really took off. The arrival of sprog number one which soon required a bedroom of its own saw the loss of my darkroom and that was the end of it.

...... occasional empty turntable pits, perhaps the basis of a Volume 3? Barnstaple 1976.

If the railways had moved on by the mid 1970s so had all of us likely lads. Trainspotting seemed confined to childhood memories and even the motorbikes had long gone, for by now we were all married with mortgages to pay. So it seemed fitting that some ten years on after trainspotting's demise a great wave of nostalgia swept over us and we indulged ourselves in shed bashing excursions but without the sheds. Iris only managed one such excursion, it takes a lot to become enthused over a pile of bricks, the odd rail and the occasional empty turntable pit.

By comparison even Barry had its attractions. Following on from my 'great accident', Paul Wells and I caught the train bug and went on our way photographing the railway scene for many years. For the others they had truly moved on. One saving grace through this 'second awakening' was that terminal stations seemed a good option for photography being full of interest, trains there are a plenty and so the odd steam special was caught on film or even indulged in. This lost opportunity in the 1960s had always grieved me, so please excuse me for now including some latter day images. Please note the word 'images', as some have been mildly digitally enhanced to remove our modern day obsession with Health & Safety. Being now promoted to grumpy old man status I don't do the silly excesses of Health & Safety and can't cope with them so I think my 'enhanced' pictures are the better for it.

Just told you, so that you know. I leave it to you to spot the 'enhancements', however I offer no prizes.

The 'King' returns to the Paddington main line hauling a special train to Didcot celebrating 125 years of Paddington station.
West Drayton 1st March 1979.

Plate 354. No.7029 *Clun Castle*　　　　　May 1988　　　　　　　　Pentax KX

Plate 355. No.7029 *Clun Castle*　May 1988　　　　Pentax KX

Inset: Old Oak Common open day, 20th September 1981. 'Castle' class No.5051 *Earl Bathurst* and BR '9F' No.92220 *Evening Star* running shuttle trains between Paddington and Old Oak.

'Castle' class No.7029 *Clun Castle* had just worked into Marylebone station with 'The Chilternian' in May 1988. Despite a few high-viz jackets about there was still sufficient atmosphere to enjoy the moment especially with the old, albeit, blue diesel multiple stock. Both are rear views as *Clun Castle* had a silly buffer beam mounted headboard, no disrespect to its creator that made it . . . but it just didn't look right.

Plate 358. 30777 *Sir Lamiel*   April 1995   Pentax KX

Plate 357. Nos. 828 (30828) & 30777 *Sir Lamiel*   April 1995   Pentax KX

A interesting rail tour organised in April 1995 from Waterloo to Southampton Docks, then round to Portsmouth and double headed back to Victoria. Sadly Portsmouth Harbour station was closed due to major maintenance work. 'King Arthur' class No.30777 waits for the 'off' at Waterloo and despite the new EMU and high rise office block enough of the station remains to give the right feel. On return to Victoria our 'King Arthur' sits behind 'S15' class No.828 (30828) which make a fine pair in a period, if very clean, setting. Route discs were all present and correct.

Plate 358. No.35028 *Clan Line*   May 1995   Pentax KX

Chasing up steam hauled boat train timings proved difficult at times, but this one worked out successfully. Photographed in May 1995 'Merchant Navy' class No.35028 *Clan Line* works out of Victoria station with the Down 'Ocean Liner Express', smoke box headboard in correct BR style. It certainly was worth the time and effort in photographing this train, not so much luck in going down to Southampton Docks on another occasion to capture a steam hauled boat train arrival. A dismally painted Class 47 turned up!

Plate 359. No.34045 *Ottery St. Mary* (34027)   October 2002   Pentax KX

Plate 360. No.34045 *Ottery St. Mary* (34027)   October 2002   Pentax KX

Victoria station again, this time at the crack of dawn for the Railway Touring Company organised London to Paris by steam and return over the weekend of the 12/13th October 2002. 'West Country' class No.34027 *Taw Valley* was re-dressed as No.34045 *Ottery St. Mary* for the occasion and a suitable SNCF Nord Pacific was provided over the other side. A wonderful trip all round, but with no rail connections at Dover and Calais, and four hundred foot passengers to organise perhaps a reason why this special trip has never been repeated.

Plate 361. No.60009 *Union of South Africa*   October 1994   Pentax KX

Plate 362. No.4468 *Mallard* (60022)   October 1986   Pentax KX

A fine view of 'A4' class No.60009 *Union of South Africa* pulling out of King's Cross station. Not exactly, she's backing her train in for the *Steam Railway* magazine's 'First A4 back to the Cross' trip to the Nene Valley Railway on the 29th October 1994. Overhead wires and new buildings all round . . . whatever happened to York Road platform? At least our 'A4' at Marylebone station on the 12th October 1986 No.4468 (60022) *Mallard* looks at home, and she had Sir Nigel Gresley for company on the opposite platform both seemingly working 'The Shakespeare Limited'.

Plate 363. No.92220 *Evening Star*   September 1981   Pentax KX

Plate 364 - FULL STOP

Last picture goes to the last steam engine built. BR Standard Class 9F No.92220 *Evening Star* taking her part in the Old Oak Common Open Day shuttle trains with 'Castle' class *Earl Bathurst* during September 1981. A grand effort on my part to get to Paddington that day only to find the steam shuttles restricted to the end of the very long Platform One. Now the man on the footplate with the trilby hat reminds me of another trilby hat seen some eighteen years earlier. Plate 8. Last 'King' Run 1963.

POSTSCRIPT

By the mid 1960s motorbikes and the 'café racer' image had overtaken us. Our motley collection of motorbikes had had their handlebars turned upside down, mudguards cut away and silencers debaffled, this didn't actually make them go any faster but at least they looked and sounded that way. With a change of image to leather jackets etc we gravitated to local transport 'caffs' or met up at the Polish War Memorial on the Western Avenue near Greenford. Most evenings were spent at such places arguing over road tests etc. and we all had our dream bikes and mine was always a BSA 499cc single cylinder Gold Star Clubman. This came to fruition on my nineteenth birthday, a 1961 model at £180, care of my auntie. Mum was not best pleased and dad kept his thoughts to himself. This was the summer of 1964 and a Gold Star although now past its peak in the hierarchy of café racers was still a well respected machine. You could make grand entrances and exits at transport 'caffs' on a Gold Star, and running on Castrol R racing oil make for a grand smell as well. However it wasn't that long before white van man had allowed me the privilege of driving straight into him and whilst waiting the Gold Star's return I met up again with Buster my old train spotting chum.

He was now wildly enthusiastic about motor cycle road racing, something which had passed us by. We all assumed we were doing this racing thing anyway, we had the Ace 'caff' on the North Circular and all the twisty bits up to the Busy Bee near Watford. Buster's own motorcycling days had ended in spectacular style and he now owned a battered Austin A55 van with little in the way of suspension. So it was we found our way bouncing to the Brands Hatch road race opener of 1965. Seeing all the stars scratching round passed me by but watching a race for road bikes

The Busy Bee transport 'caff', early 1960s.
(Courtesy the Busy Bee Motorcycle Club)

and all the frantic activity in the paddock I knew then and there that I wanted to be on the inside of the fence. As for the North Circular road, you could keep it. On the Goldie's return roads took on a totally new meaning and everything including roundabouts had to be taken on the racing line, sometimes with startling results. Being last into a bend and first out took on a new meaning. Attempts at tuning our bikes were undertaken spending hours polishing piston crowns and porting. Much money was spent by myself on a very expensive high compression piston, this impressed both my mates and myself but I was less impressed when it seized up shortly after fitting it. Undeterred my camshafts were sent of for reprofiling - racing style. On their return I was so horrified to find that their profile now resembled square biscuit tins that I wasn't going to use them. Lucky I did 'cos married to my mate Ginger's silencer they transformed the bike, although at a stroke rendering it near useless for the road. Ginger by the way had spent all of one day knocking out the baffles from his own Goldie's silencer with his mothers broom handle. Now in the world of motorbikes a Gold Star is famous for its 'twitter' on the exhaust note. On our arrival Ginger was distraught as his bike had now lost its twitter and from his point of view a twitterless Gold Star was beyond belief. I quickly seized the opportunity to try Ginger's latest mod as my own night time trials running on an open megaphone had ended in failure. Being at the time totally ignorant regarding the mystic art of carburettor tuning and ignition timing I suppose it was more luck than judgement that my biscuit tin cams worked well with Ginger's now open silencer. Still, much to the neighbours dismay, I was now the owner of a quite fast but VERY noisy Gold Star.

A second hand race approved 'pudding basin' crash helmet was acquired, safety being of an understandable low priority and I was ready for the 'off' in my racing career. Well by the end of the 1966 racing season I'd realised that I was nothing like ready for the 'off'. Today it would be

Ted Reading, Silverstone 1966.

called a 'learning curve' The trouble was that even with help from my dad competition work taxed my mechanical skills to the absolute limit and sadly all my efforts in burning the midnight oil and conning Buster to be my race transport were to end in tears and frustration. I stumbled through four race meetings and two sprints but all my training down the North Circular road had come to nought.

The old Goldie might not have been the most competitive of machines but it was an achievement to actually finish two races, albeit more at the back than the front. Contact breaker failure and to literally vanish into a corn field accounting for the other two..

Sprinting was no better as I came up against something called 'gearing'. This was something of a mystery to me, but I quickly found out that my bikes 'gearing' was pretty well useless for both sprinting or road racing.

By the end of 1966 Buster decided that racing ought to be more exciting than this and sold me the van for £15 - not that I had a car licence, but that's another story. During the year I had occasionally ridden the bike to race tracks and it became apparent that 'race transport' was vital.

For 1967 both former trainspotting chums Paul Wells and John Durrant decided to join me at this motorcycle racing business, Peter Askey thinking the better of it. Things seemed to be going much the same as before, the harder I tried the more erratic the bike seemed till I discovered something called 'swinging arm bushes' and mine were clapped out. Once this little problem was sorted out I slowly started to improve.

The race meetings we entered at were at club level and my bike was in production, or road trim, and production races were all kick start affairs. I generally had no problems in firing the bike up until my public debut at a Crystal Palace meeting. With the start line area packed with eager spectators I totally fluffed it in front of a packed audience. Bloody typical. Eventually I got away but it was all to late and once again I was relegated to the back of the field.

To put it mildly I was somewhat fed up, but I wasn't to know that within a few weeks everything would go right. It has often been said that every dog has his day and mine was at Snetterton race track, near Norwich in September. The day started wet but cleared, the entry was smaller than usual and the top man in my class, for 500cc machines, had blown up his Triumph Daytona in practise. The old Goldie went like a song pulling around 7400rpm on a 5.0 top gear giving around 115mph. I'd even found out about gearing! My bike

Ted Reading, John Durrant and Paul Wells.
Three trainspotters go motorcycle road racing. Brands Hatch 1967.

and I were in perfect harmony. We went like a proverbial train. None of the other bikes in my class could touch me. Triumphs and Velocettes were blown off in no uncertain terms. I spent the entire race mixing it with a chap on a 1000cc Vincent, a machine that totally saw me off down the straights but seemingly requiring nerves of steel to propel it around the corners. Talk about a camel just how he stayed on it was a miracle and me a few feet behind his chuff. Sad to say although I did get past him it didn't stay that way and he got the better of me relegating me to seventh place

overall, but first 500 home. Still got the mug to prove it, but I didn't get my name in the results.

The last meeting of the year, again at Snetterton, in October put me in my place good and proper. Although I put up a faster race time I only managed twelfth place overall and fifth 500 home. After that it was downhill all the way. During the winter of 1967/68 instead of burning even more of the midnight oil I had been swayed into another lifestyle of beer, dance halls and of all things a suit.

No bad thing though as I met Iris.

Paul Wells, Brands Hatch 1967.

However the immediate effect of all these distractions was a late start to the 1968 season culminating in a serious prang which laid the Goldie up for most of the year. On resurrection she suffered serious ignition problems, the magneto having given up the ghost. The end of my Goldie sort of coincided with the end of steam on BR. Mum kept back the newspapers to show me but sadly it just didn't register.

John Durrant packed up after a year while Paul Wells carried on for a few years and proved to be the fastest of us all but continual mechanical problems put an end to it. Competitive sport, like anything you put your heart and soul into, is totally demanding and never cheap.

By now interest and finances were at a low ebb so by 1970 the dear old Goldie had been exchanged for a racing version. We plodded round for a few times but to be honest I had lost all interest and was simply going through the motions. Selling it turned out to be quite an event. Having found a prospective buyer he wanted to test ride it so I took him and his mate who had just built up a Velocette special down to Brands Hatch. All went well until they went out together. Can't remember if the Goldie went down first or if the Velo did, but it was a very subdued drive home. Anyway he bought the bike and I retired . . . for a while anyway.

By August 1968 main line steam on British Railways had finished. My Gold Star
lasted another month before that too had its final run at Snetterton
in September 1968.